THE
HAPPY
GOSPEL!

+

THE
HAPPY
GOSPEL!

effortless union with a
HAPPY GOD
BENJAMIN DUNN

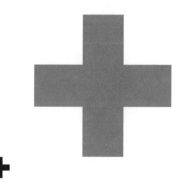

DESTINY IMAGE® PUBLISHERS, INC.

P.O. Box 310, Shippensburg, PA 17257-0310

"Speaking to the Purposes of God for This Generation and for the Generations to Come."

This book and all other Destiny Image, Revival Press, Mercy Place, Fresh Bread, Destiny Image Fiction, and Treasure House books are available at Christian bookstores and distributors worldwide.

For a U.S. bookstore nearest you, call 1-800-722-6774.

For more information on foreign distributors, call 717-532-3040.

Or reach us on the Internet: www.destinyimage.com

Trade Paper ISBN 13: 978-0-7684-3704-1
Hardcover ISBN 13: 978-0-7684-3705-8
Large Print ISBN 13: 978-0-7684-3706-5
Ebook ISBN 13: 978-0-7684-9019-0

For Worldwide Distribution, Printed in the U.S.A.

1 2 3 4 5 6 7 8 / 15 14 13 12 11

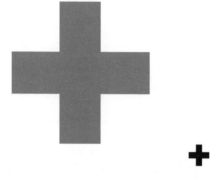

ENDORSEMENTS

ENDORSEMENTS

Benjamin Dunn has stumbled on the only force to be reckoned with in this universe: the cross of our Lord Jesus Christ and all of its implications. While religion offers dull, sedative, boring theories, Benjamin knows the real Gospel can be nothing less than a radical affectionate enjoyment of the cross. And only a joyful public expression of the finished work of the cross can even begin to capture and hold the hearts and minds of this next generation.

Somewhere, somehow, Benjamin heard the whisper of the Spirit nudging him in a totally new direction, and with breath-less awe and childlike wonder he "believed." This believing is what will begin to unfold in these pages. Although it will never come to an end, it promises to leave you scandalized and breathless.

On a more practical side, my husband and I have been

privileged to travel with Ben and Stephanie all around the world. I have seen him time after time pour out liquid love from the fullness of his heart to the forgotten ones—the ones society no longer accepts. I have witnessed him serenade a poor, toothless gypsy woman until she smiled like a girl again. I have watched him touch the lepers of India getting them to sing, dance, and even clap hands that are no longer there. I have seen him on his knees with guitar in hand in garbage dumps worldwide singing private love songs to those who have nearly lost hope. I have seen him frolic in the streets of the slums with the tangible presence of the love of God. This happy Gospel that he carries is no joke! It has joyful arms and legs and a brilliant voice, and it looks like Benjamin Dunn.

GEORGIAN AND WINNIE BANOV+
Global Celebration

This new book by Benjamin Dunn has completely caught me off guard, as it is one of the most well-written, well-versed books I've read in a long time. Benjamin's revelations of the new creation realities not only expose the true nature and hidden design of humanity, but also reveal the blissful heart of God for His most loved creation…us. In the pages of this book, you will find God's blueprint for us to live a happy, triumphant, overcoming life and the joy that comes in knowing the reality of Christ in us. I recommend this book to all who are looking for more and thirsting for the deep things of God.

I've personally known Benjamin and Stephanie for several years now and not only is Benjamin a talented musician, songwriter, and author, but he is a dear friend.

JEFF JANSEN+
Global Fire Ministries

The Happy Gospel is a book that reveals the ways of a loving Father. Benjamin has done a great job in opening to us the full *joy* of the Gospel. This book will help you dive into the heavenly joy and happiness that is yours to experience now. Because of what Jesus did on the cross, we can live with a happy heart and be joyful. Thank you, Benjamin, for this book that is so important and timely.

BENI JOHNSON, PASTOR+
Bethel Church, Redding, California
Author, *The Happy Intercessor*

It has been our joy and privilege to have Benjamin minister with us in our churches in the bush of Mozambique. He has an extraordinary gift of love, which shows itself in the way he connects with people of many cultures. Ben is an amazing musician and he carries a contagious passion for Jesus.

HEIDI BAKER, PH.D.+
Founding Director, Iris Ministries, Inc.

As Benjamin's pastor for many years, I can tell you that Christ does indeed fully possess him in an intoxicating manner, and the revelation in this book can only lead you to one conclusion: I, too, must be a drinker of this grace.

ERIC HANSEN, LEAD PASTOR+
IWorship Center, Springfield, Illinois

Benjamin is one of the happiest people I know. His life is a song of joy that sparkles with the uncreated light of Heaven. You are about to read some of the lyrics and some of the heartbeat behind Ben's euphoria. Warning—this book is full of contagious joy and shocking perspectives on the *great salvation* that has been lavished upon us through the cross. If you want to be infected with Heaven's love, then read on; or rather, drink in these liquid, light, love words.

CHARLES AND ANN STOCK, LEAD PASTORS+
Life Center International, Harrisburg, Pennsylvania
Clear River Network

Enjoy a deep drink of the Gospel as Benjamin Dunn unfolds the life-altering paradigms of grace in this work. The sweet simplicity of the cross confounds preachers and prophets alike in today's doldrum world of do-it-yourself Christianity. But Benjamin is bringing a radical revelation that is beyond timely—it is essential for today's church.

For years, Benjamin and I have partnered closely in ministry both as friends and co-laborers, traveling the globe on a divine quest of holy fun. I have seen him in action. I can attest that the message you read here is one that thoroughly infuses and possesses him to the core. The caliber of his character, quality of his marriage, compassion for the poor, and unspeakable joy are undeniable results of the theological foundation found in these chapters. It seems in every generation, the Lord appoints a few troublers of Israel to challenge the status quo and awaken His people to the authentic Gospel. Benjamin is a trouble maker through and through. Allow the Lord to stir you, challenge you, and delight you as Benjamin proclaims His obnoxiously happy message!

JOHN CROWDER+
Sons of Thunder Ministries & Publications
Author, *The New Mystics* and *The Ecstasy of Loving God*

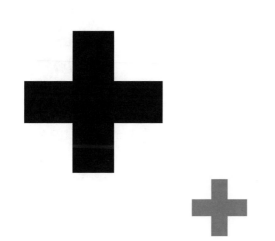

THANKS

THANKS

MY WIFE STEPHANIE+ thank you for being my love and for drinking with me from the same glorious message of the cross.

GEORGIAN AND WINNIE BANOV+ thank you for leading us to the fountain of bliss and teaching us everything! This whole book could be in your quotation marks.

SAINT PAUL THE APOSTLE+ you are my hero!

THE WRITINGS OF ADAM CLARKE+ you have been my constant companion.

ALL THE BIBLE TRANSLATORS+ for spending their lives studying and uncovering the treasures that they did.

ERIC HANSEN+ thank you for always being a wonderful encouragement and a loving pastor!

JOHN CROWDER✛ thank you for teaching me how to make footnotes and for being a perfect friend in "The Revelation."

MY LITTLE BROTHER LUKE✛ thank you for being such a perfect example of what the Gospel can do.

LEVI VINCENT✛ thank you for being an outlet for some of these revelations; our talks on the phone are priceless.

OUR SANTA CRUZ COMMUNITY✛ thank you for loving the message of the cross so much!

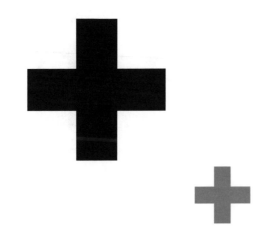

CONTENTS

+ CONTENTS

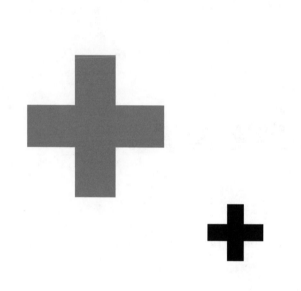

01

+ AN
INTRODUCTION

My intention in writing this book is not at all to try and cram an explanation of *all* of the wonderful goodies of the Gospel into less than two hundred pages. If I did attempt this, it would take me more than a hundred lifetimes—and a heck of a lot more espresso.

Rather, this book is an overflow of revelation that has been brewing in me for quite a while now. I simply have written what I believe.

Though some things in this book may shock and scandalize you, I know that you will come out with the breathtaking breakthrough that only the preaching of the cross can give.

I would say go ahead and let this book shake your house. If it is built upon the right foundation, it will stand. But if not, I hope you will join me in joyfully saying, "Let that old thing tumble!" knowing that God, of course, will make everything new for you.

Through my love and passion for the Word, and through many talks with my wife and great friends, I have stumbled into a massive vineyard. The specific source of this vineyard's goodness is its unusual winepress—the cross of Christ, from where all of the Gospel's vintages flow.

I personally, maybe rather selfishly, have been enjoying and feasting upon this vineyard for myself for some time now, and when I became brim-full and could hold no more, out came this book.

My cup has overflowed!

Though the contents of this vintage are rich and intoxicating, I know that it can only get better with time. So, in saying that, I feel it necessary to state that this is one of many volumes on a subject that only eternity can hold.

This is *The Happy Gospel!*

02

+ **EXPLANATION** OF BIBLE TRANSLATIONS

The following is an explanation of the many different translations of the Bible that are used in this book. I absolutely love translations, and I have spent much time and effort compiling a wonderful trove of them in my home library. Here are the ones that were used in this book:

AMPLIFIED+ *The Amplified Bible* (Frances Siewert). Grand Rapids: Zondervan Publishing House, 1965.

ANCIENT ROOTS+ *Ancient Roots Translinear Bible* (A. Frances Werner). ARTB LLC 2005, 2006.

A.S. WAY+ *Letters of Paul, Hebrews and the Book of Psalms* (Author S. Way). Grand Rapids: Kregel Publications, 1981.

BARCLAY+ *The New Testament, A New Translation* (William Barclay). London: Collins Clear-Type Press, 1968.

BERKELEY+ *The Holy Bible, the Berkeley Version In Modern English* (Gerrit Verkuyl). Grand Rapids: Zondervan Publishing House, 1959.

CONYBEARE+ *The Life and Epistles of St. Paul* (W.J. Conybeare, J.S. Howson). Grand Rapids: Wm. B. Eerdmans Publishing Company, 1978.

COTTON PATCH+ *Cotton Patch Version* (Clarence Jordan). New York: Association Press, various dates.

DISTILLED+ *The Distilled Bible* (Roy Greenhill). Stone Mountain: P. Benjamin Publishers, 1980.

DARBY+ *The Holy Scriptures, A New Translation From the Original Languages* (J.N. Darby). Lancing, Sussex: Kingston Bible Trust, 1980.

DOUAY-RHEIMS+ *The Douay-Rheims Bible*, from the Latin Vulgate into English. The New Testament was published in one volume with extensive commentary and notes in 1582.

ERV+ *The New Testament of Our Lord and Saviour Jesus Christ* (C.J. Ellicott, et. al.). Oxford: Oxford University Press, 1881.

EXEGESES+ *Exegeses Bible* (Herb Jahn), 1992.

F.F. BRUCE+ *An Expanded Paraphrase of the Epistles of*

Paul (F.F. Bruce). Palm Springs, CA: Ronald N. Haynes Publishers, Inc., 1981.

GOD'S WORD+ *GOD'S WORD Translation*. God's Word to the Nations, 1995.

HEART OF PAUL+ *The Heart of Paul* (Ben Campbell Johnson). Waco, TX: Word Books, 1976.

JERUSALEM BIBLE+ *The Jerusalem Bible*. New York: Doubleday & Company, Inc., 1968.

KNOX+ *The New Testament of Our Lord and Saviour Jesus Christ* (Ronald A. Knox). New York: Sheed & Ward, 1947.

LAMSA+ *The Holy Bible From Ancient Eastern Manuscripts* (George M. Lamsa). Philadelphia: A.J. Holman Company, 1957.

LITV+ *The Literal Translation of the Holy Bible* (Jay P. Green, Sr.), Sovereign Grace Publishers, 1976–2000.

MESSAGE+ *The Message: The New Testament in Contemporary English* (Eugene H. Peterson). Colorado Springs: NavPress, 1993.

MOFFATT+ *The Bible, A New Translation* (James Moffatt). New York: Harper & Row, Publishers, 1954.

NEB+ *The New English Bible*. New York: Oxford University Press, 1971.

PHILLIPS+ *The New Testament in Modern English* (J.B. Phillips). New York: The Macmillan Company, 1972.

ROTHERHAM+ *The Emphasized Bible* (Joseph B. Rotherham). Grand Rapids: Kregel Publications, 1959.

SEPTUAGINT+ *A New English Translation of the Septuagint*. New York: Oxford University Press, 2007.

STEVENS+ *The Epistles of Paul in Modern English* (George Barker Stevens). Wheaton, IL: Verploegh Editions, 1980.

TCNT+ *Twentieth Century New Testament*. Cambridge, United Kingdom: Tyndale House, 1904.

WUEST+ *Wuest's Expanded Translation of the Greek New Testament* (Kenneth S. Wuest). Grand Rapids: Wm. B. Eerdmans Publishing Company, 1959.

WEYMOUTH+ *The New Testament in Modern Speech* (Richard Francis Weymouth). Boston: The Pilgrim Press, n.d.

WILLIAMS+ *The New Testament in the Language of the People* (Charles B. Williams). Chicago: Moody Press, 1937.

WYCLIFFE+ *Wycliffe's New Testament*: a modern-spelling edition of their 14th century Middle English translation; the first complete English vernacular version, with an introduction by Terence P. Noble. (John Wycliffe and John Purvey). Vancouver: T.P. Noble, 2001.

YOUNG'S LITERAL TRANSLATION+ *Young's Literal Translation of the Holy Bible* (Robert Young). Grand Rapids: Baker Book House, 1976.

If I have put only the Scripture reference and not the translation in the note, it is either because I have used only part of the Scripture as part of my sentence, or that I wanted to convey only the general idea of the verse within the sentence while still wanting to give reference to it.

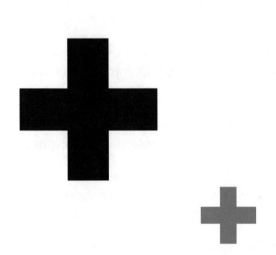

03

+REDEFINING OUR WORDS

Following are some definitions of terms and words I have used in this book that I feel would be very useful to know and to be given a fresh look. I have used Scripture, commentaries, Greek lexicons, and dictionaries to define and explain the meanings; these mostly have shaped my writing language.

Though some of these words have been predefined for most of us and are common in Christian and modern usage, I feel it necessary to redefine or at least rediscover some of their purer definitions so that these words will again have their desired effect upon our hearts.

Read these definitions and let the Lord give you a framework for joyful salvation. Let Him teach you His language.

GOSPEL+

I use the word *Gospel* not in the sense of "the four Gospels" but mostly in the sense of the revealing of salvation through the work of Christ on the cross, which is expounded, amplified, and focused on mainly in the epistles of Paul.

The glad-message of the glory of the happy God.[1] The glad tidings of salvation through Christ; the proclamation of the grace of God manifested and pledged in Christ.[2]

GRACE+

The divine influence upon the heart and its reflection in the life, including gratitude. Total undeserved divine favor, by which man is saved.[3]

Grace is not just the kindness or mercy that is shown by the Lord when one is in a fallen condition, but Grace is also the influence that keeps one from falling.

FAITH+

Trust. A firm persuasion produced by God's infinite goodness. A childlike response to God's wonderful love and works.[4] It is also a gift.[5]

SALVATION+

The spiritual and eternal deliverance granted immediately by God to those who accept His conditions of repentance and faith in the Lord Jesus.[6] It is not earned but is a gift.[7]

The present experience of God's power to deliver from the bondage of sin.[8]

SIN+

Sin is personified as a slave master in the epistles of Paul.[9] It is an inward element producing evil acts.[10] A governing principle or power.[11]

FLESH+

When I use this word, I don't mean flesh in the sense of "the body" of men or animals, or as in the animated, organized matter that all creatures share, which is not evil at all, but I use it in the sinful sense, meaning the sinful nature.[12] The whole, corrupt, carnal nature with its passions and lusts.[13] The unregenerate state of men that was destroyed or cut away by Christ at salvation.

"The Flesh," "Old-Man," "Sinful-Self" and "Sin-Nature" are all different terms to describe the same unregenerate state, and all fall under this definition.

RIGHTEOUS/RIGHTEOUSNESS+

Uprightness and right standing with God.[14] The state of him who is as he ought to be.[15]

JUSTIFIED/JUSTIFICATION+

Declared or rendered righteous apart from the works of the Law or self-works.[16]

SANCTIFICATION/SANCTIFIED+

Sanctification is a person—who is Christ Himself. Holiness and purification. The effect of being consecrated unto God.[17] It is the divine act preceding the acceptance of the Gospel by the individual.[18]

WORKS/SELF-WORKS+

As opposed to "fruit of the Spirit."[19] Works, deeds, or efforts devoid of that life which has its source in God. The attempt to gain God's approval apart from faith.

FRUIT OF THE SPIRIT+

The work that the Holy Spirit's presence accomplishes within and through the believer.[20]

RELIGION+

Used in the sense of being in contrast to true worship and "pure religion,"[21] which come from the heart.

External ordinances and disciplines; a form of godliness that does not come from within the heart.

BLISS+

Extreme happiness.[22] The ecstasy of salvation; spiritual joy.[23]

ECSTASY+

Intense joy and delight. A state of emotion so intense that one is carried beyond rational thought and self-control.[24]

A throwing of the mind out of its normal state, alienation of mind, whether such as makes a lunatic or that of a man who by some sudden emotion is transported, as it were, out of himself, so that in this rapt condition, although he is awake, his mind is drawn off from all surrounding objects and wholly fixed on things divine, so that he sees nothing but the forms and images lying within and thinks that he perceives with his bodily eyes and ears realities shown him by God.[25]

GOD+

The English word *God* has Anglo-Saxon origins, and it seems that the words *good* and *God* were correlative terms.

> The Good Being, a fountain of infinite benevolence and beneficence towards His creatures. The eternal, independent, and self-existent Being: the Being whose purposes and actions spring from Himself, without foreign motive or influence: He who is absolute in dominion; the most pure, the most simple, and the most spiritual of all essences; true, and holy: the cause of all being, the upholder of all things; infinitely happy, because infinitely perfect; and eternally self-sufficient, needing nothing that He has made: illimitable in His immensity, inconceivable in His mode of existence, and indescribable in His essence; known fully only to Himself, because an infinite mind can be fully apprehended only by itself.
>
> In a word, a Being who, from His infinite wisdom, cannot err or be deceived; and who, from His infinite goodness, can do nothing but what is eternally just, right, and kind.
>
> Reader, such is the God of the Bible; but how

widely different from the God of most human creeds and apprehensions![26]

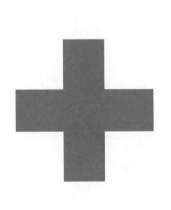

04

+THE GLAD-MESSAGE OF THE HAPPY GOD

You might be thinking, *The Happy Gospel? Are you kidding me?*

I know this may be a shock, but just hold on; it's going to be OK!

When most people hear the word *Gospel,* they seldom think *happy*.

Because of the poison of religion and its perversions, the word *Gospel* is seldom spoken with the idea of its goodness and gladness.

When I hear the word *Gospel*, though, it thrills my emotions to frenzy. It makes my heart leap like a spring lamb. For me, the

Gospel is *my everything* because I have tasted of the Source of its gladness.

I, like Paul, have been "*set apart for its publishing.*" [27]

I am "*a bondslave by nature, belonging to Christ Jesus, an ambassador by divine summons, permanently separated to God's good news.*"[28]

I am permanently separated to boast and take joy in nothing else, for nothing but the Gospel carries the dose of joy that my heart requires.

The Gospel is the Glad-Message!

That is its simplest definition.

It is "*...the glad-message of the happy God*"[29] as Rotherham translates it.

The nature of the Gospel is eternal gladness. Joy is most certainly its native tongue.

> We must earnestly endeavor to learn this practice, or at the least to attain to some knowledge thereof; and we must raise up ourselves with this consideration—that the gospel is nothing else but laughter and joy. —Martin Luther[30]

The focus of this *Happy Message* is and will always be the nature of who God is and the nature of what He has accomplished for humanity through His Son, Jesus the Christ.

This message to humanity is infinitely blissful and glad, for in it we find the cure for fallen humankind.

It offers a curse-free life—a happy life!

The Gospel itself is the drink that every heart longs for. It lifts man from his wretched and sinful state into the limitless heights of happiness and holiness found only in salvation.

"The Gospel is centered in God's Son" [31] and tells of a new existence given graciously to all who believe and trust in its power.

When you encounter the pure and true Gospel, you encounter something from another realm. It will hit you like a ton of bricks. Its goodness instantly disintegrates all of your tainted, preconceived ideas about Christianity. It revolutionizes you and scandalizes everything that you ever heard, or maybe even believed, about Christ and His work on the cross.

Does this sound foreign? When you think of the Gospel, do you see it in such light and joy?

If not, would you like to think of it that way?

I would like to challenge you to dig deep into the core of what you know as "the Gospel," and see if you find the same as I have.

Shall you find the same treasure?

The truth is that there are many non-gospels that are in opposition to God's Good News. [32]

These pretend to be God's message, but none of these can or will have the same effect as the true Gospel upon the heart of the believer. None can produce the heart satisfaction and endless peace that only the true Good News can procure.

When this message is declared, it does not leave a person at the altar in a puddle of tears, feeling unworthy and pitiful.

No. In fact, when preached in its purity, the glorious Gospel lifts people from the garbage dumps of sin and seats them in heavenly places with Christ.

It leaves humanity with a realization that there was an inestimable cost paid to make them worthy.

The Gospel opens the door to a new reality. It leaves us with beauty in trade for ashes. Tears are turned into wine; depression is turned into dancing.

The Gospel leads people to repentance, not because of the fear of eternal punishment, but because of the promise of eternal bliss!

It is the goodness of God that leads a man to repent. It is His divine pleasures that entices salvation.

In the Gospel, we see the greatest gift ever given to the world—the gift of Christ.

He was sent not to condemn the human race, but to save it from a lifeless existence separated from God.

He was sent to save us from sin and its sting in this life!

The Gospel is the shocking offer of instantaneous freedom from sin. It is the voice of the Lord that speaks into the darkness and turns it into light.

It transforms humanity from wretched to worthy.

To know the Gospel as anything less than this is tragic. Unless it is known and drunk down in its entirety, its benefits will never be realized.

It has to be seen that the Gospel is a Gospel of extreme grace. It holds infinitely more grace than we could ever dream or imagine.

When we see the promises offered in the Gospel, it leaves us breathless. We are clueless when it comes to the reality of the goodness and grace that the Gospel offers us.

> Indeed, if we consider the unblushing promises of reward and the staggering nature of the rewards promised in the Gospels, it would seem that Our Lord finds our desires not strong, but too weak. We are half-hearted creatures, fooling about with drink and sex and ambition when infinite joy is offered us, like an ignorant child who wants to go on making mud pies in a slum because he cannot imagine what is meant by the offer of a holiday at the sea.[33]

The Gospel offers a drink of grace that none could afford, yet it asks for nothing in return.

> ...come, buy and eat! Yes, come, buy [priceless, spiritual] wine and milk without money and without price [simply for the self-surrender that accepts the blessing].[34]

When this drink of grace has been drunk, we are left under its divine influence. In fact, that is the definition of grace: "*the divine influence upon the heart, and its reflection in the life.*"[35]

This possession by grace illustrates itself by outward expressions of joy.

The glorious Gospel was intended and can only be perfectly communicated in this way—through public displays of divine affection.

The Gospel fills us with God's pleasure and makes the world jealous, and there is nothing more persuasive than a believer enjoying God!

That's what we were created for!

The Westminster Larger Catechism asks:

> What is the chief and highest end of man? And answers: Man's chief and highest end is to glorify God, and to fully enjoy him forever.[36]

Only the glorious Gospel, the Good News of what Christ has done for us on the cross, can provide a way for people to both glorify God and enjoy Him forever.

From every dimension, the Gospel beams pure joy. This joy is the joy of salvation from the former life.

This news truly is good!

Let's dig into the source of the Gospel's goodness and find its treasures.

Let's lock ourselves in the cellar of the words of Paul for a while and see what vintage we might find.

> The words of Paul are living creatures, and have hands and feet. —Martin Luther

Let us have an encounter with those living creatures found in the Gospel.

We may, like Martin Luther, find a revolution of laughter and joy.

+ WINE IS THE SYMBOL of the New Testament

The Gospel is the "glad message" because it offers a way out of sin through the sacrifice of Christ. It offers the only exodus from that pitiful existence of separation from God.

When one drinks of the sacrifice of Christ, he or she partakes of the cup of salvation and the New Covenant. It's amazing that many Christians have no clue of the joy offered in this cup.

I've had many people ask me, "Why all this talk of wine and drinking?"

Well, I will let the Lord Himself, in His own wonderful words, answer that question:

> *And He took the cup, and gave thanks, and gave it to them, saying, Drink ye all of it; for this is My blood of the new testament, which is shed for many for the remission of sins.* [37]

This is probably one of the loudest messages that Jesus speaks within the four Gospels.

He says, *"This is my blood of the new testament."*

What do you suppose was in that cup?

Water? Grape juice?

No, it was wine!

The only thing that Jesus uses to describe His blood is wine. He could have used any substance on Earth, but He uses wine.

Why?

Because wine is the only thing that can communicate the intense joy and inebriation that fills the heart when salvation's cup is drunk.

Jesus describes the New Covenant as something supremely intoxicating!

Usually when a covenant is made between two parties, it involves certain requirements to be met between the two who are in covenant together.

I was looking at this Scripture and it hit me!

Jesus said, *"Drink it."*

My part in the covenant is to drink of what He has done!

Christianity consists of drinking from the blood of Christ and feasting upon His body. Unless we drink His blood and eat His body, we have no life in us.

Jesus was in no way promoting cannibalism in this statement; He was telling us where to find true life.

The life is in the blood![38] Christ was showing us that all spiritual life and joy comes from His sacrifice.

When we drink the wine of this New Covenant, we become intoxicated and yet sober at the same time.

We sober up from the fantasy of an independent existence outside of God, which can only produce sinfulness, and become overcome by the joy of our dependence upon and union with Christ.

Psalm 23 in the Douay-Rheims Translation says:

> *And my chalice which inebriateth me, how goodly is it!*[39]

> ...the intoxication of the Lord's cup and blood is not such as is the intoxication of the

world's wine, since the Holy Spirit said in the Psalm, "Thy inebriating cup." He added, "how excellent it is," because doubtless the Lord's cup so inebriates them that drink, that it makes them sober; it restores their minds to spiritual wisdom; that each one recovers from that flavor of the world to the understanding of God; and in the same way, that by that common wine the mind is dissolved, and the soul relaxed, and all sadness is laid aside, so, when the blood of the Lord and the cup of salvation have been drunk, the memory of the old man is laid aside, and there arises an oblivion of the former worldly conversation, and the sorrowful and sad breast which before was oppressed by tormenting sins is eased by the joy of the divine mercy.[40]

When we drink from the cup of the Lord, we are partaking of His sacrifice. We are drinking the freedom He has provided for us, and this is intoxicating!

Drink from this cup and let the Gospel intoxicate you like it did Martin Luther and the reformers.

It is said that:

The Reformation was a time when men went blind, staggering drunk because they had discovered, in the dusty basement of late medievalism, a whole cellarful of fifteen-hundred-year-old, two-hundred-proof grace—of bottle after bottle of pure distillate of Scripture, one sip of which would convince anyone that God saves us single-handedly.

The word of the gospel—after all those centuries of trying to lift yourself into heaven by worrying about the perfection of your bootstraps— suddenly turned out to be a flat announcement that the saved were home free before they started....

Grace has to be drunk straight: no water, no ice, and certainly no ginger ale....[41]

+ ENVY of the Fathers and of the Angels

Inside the Old Testament, we find endless rivers running wildly through every page, all of them flowing and secretly drawing us into the vast ocean of the reality of Christ. Every word written screams His glorious name.

Absolutely every character and story is a shadow cast by the One who was to come and His Kingdom. Characters, though before the time of Christ, entered into faith and saw Him. Every miracle, sign, wonder, and prophecy reverberated His approaching.

They all looked toward the future when the coming of the Messiah would usher in a new age of God among us, a day when Immanuel would come to the hearts of all.

They saw and declared what was to come; yet, we declare what is here.

He has come!

They saw and emulated as types and shadows the things that

we now enjoy as a reality. Christ has emerged from the shadows and has publicly declared His undying love for all humankind through His death upon the cross.

With His *"explosion out from among the dead"* [42] in His resurrection, He has begun His glorious Kingdom, to reign sovereign in our hearts—a marvelous new Kingdom centered on a people consumed by the King of Glory.

We are a people indwelt by God!

Abraham saw this day, Christ's day,[43] and jumped for joy.[44] Now this Happy Gospel has been fully disclosed to us.

Moses sang of His coming, David wrote of His mercies, all the prophets trumpeted His arrival. Yet, we have drunk of Him.

Because we have this Gospel's fullness, we have become the envy of the fathers. The great cloud of witnesses long to peek into what we now enjoy.

We are even the envy of the angels!

> *Concerning which salvation prophets conducted an exhaustive inquiry and search, those who prophesied concerning the particular grace destined for you…*
>
> *…which things angels have a passionate desire to stoop way down and look into [like the cherubim above the mercy seat who gazed at the sprinkled blood and wondered at its meaning].* [45]

Wow, what a glorious existence we have!

We now get to see the reality of Christ, who before was casting His shadow upon the patriarchs and prophets of the Old Testament.

+ ECSTASY of the Gospel

The Gospel has fully matured and has been poured out upon us! The *ecstasy* of the Gospel.

Throughout the Bible, we find the word *ecstasy*.

I'm not talking about the street drug; I'm talking about the bliss of salvation.

The Greek word *ecstasis,*[46] which is found multiple times in the New Testament, is where we get the transliterated word **ecstasy**.

I have found many Bible translations that use this word, and I have included some of the references here for your enjoyment:

ECSTASY IN THE PSALMS+

> *There is Benjamin a youth, in **ecstasy** of mind. The princes of Judah are their leaders: the princes of Zebulon, the princes of Naphtali.* [47]

> *Unto the end, a psalm for David, in an **ecstasy**.*[48]

ECSTASY AT JESUS' BIRTH+

> *When they saw the star, they were thrilled with **ecstatic** joy.*[49]

ECSTASY AT THE MIRACLES OF JESUS+

> *And they knew him, that he it was that sat at alms at the fair gate of the temple. And they were filled with wondering, and astonishing, in that thing that befelled to him [And they were full-filled with*

*wonder, and **ecstasy**, that is losing of mind and reason, and letting of tongue, in that thing that befell to him].* [50]

*And overwhelming astonishment and **ecstasy** seized them all, and they recognized and praised and thanked God; and they were filled with and controlled by reverential fear and kept saying, We have seen wonderful and strange and incredible and unthinkable things today!* [51]

ECSTASY AT JESUS' RESURRECTION+

*And going out quickly, they fled from the tomb. And trembling and **ecstasy** took hold of them. And they told no one, not a thing, for they were afraid.* [52]

*So saying, He showed them His hands and His side. And when the disciples saw the Lord, they were filled with joy (delight, exultation, **ecstasy**, rapture).* [53]

PETER'S ECSTASY+

*And he became hungry and desired to eat. But as they were making ready an **ecstasy** came upon him.* [54]

*I was in the city of Joppa praying, and in an **ecstasy** I saw a vision, a certain vessel descending like a great sheet, let down by four corners out of heaven, and it came even to me.* [55]

I was in the city of Joppa praying, and I saw in

*an **ecstasy** of mind a vision, a certain vessel descending, as it were a great sheet let down from heaven by four corners, and it came even unto me.[56]*

ECSTASY OF PAUL+

*If we are standing outside ourselves in **ecstasy**, it is for God.[57]*

*Then when I had come back to Jerusalem and was praying in the temple [enclosure], I fell into a trance (an **ecstasy**).[58]*

And it came to pass when I had returned to Jerusalem, and as I was praying in the temple, that I became in ecstasy.[59]

ECSTASY IN JUDE+

*Now to Him Who is able to keep you without stumbling or slipping or falling, and to present [you] unblemished (blameless and faultless) before the presence of His glory in triumphant joy and exultation [with unspeakable, **ecstatic** delight].[60]*

These are just some, not all, of the references to ecstasy that I have found in the Bible.

I have come to realize that as we dive into the world of the Gospel, we find endless storehouses of pleasure reserved for believers.

In the Gospel, we find the ecstasy of salvation. It is impossible to know Christ's work on the cross and not be overwhelmed by the joy and pleasure of it.

The pleasure originally intended for humankind was the pleasure of being in union with God.

When Adam was created, he was created in the image of God.

One of the definitions of the Hebrew word for *image* is *"shadow."*[61] Man was created to be the Lord's shadow, to mimic every move like a child.

He was created with unlimited potential for joy, love, and God-likeness. He was placed into the Garden of pleasure and was given earth as a gift. His only job was to tend the Garden of pleasure and be dependent upon his creator.

When I see the picture that Genesis paints, I see a wonderful place of union, where God created man to be the object of His intense love.

God walked with man with no separation between Heaven and Earth; for in the beginning God created the heavens and the Earth at the same moment. There was no divide between the two. Heaven and Earth were intertwined into the fabric of one another.

The Lord gave to Adam to eat from any tree in the Garden, including the Tree of Life. On a side note, it always puzzles me why Adam never ate of that tree.

The only tree he was not to eat from was the tree of the knowledge of good and evil.

The Lord installed a simple directive to show man that he must trust God. It was intended to show man that though he was created in the image and likeness of God, he was still to be dependent.

Then we read that the serpent came with a temptation: if they ate of the tree, which the Lord prohibited, they would become like God.

But wait, I thought that they were already made in God's image. I thought that they were like God in every way, like His shadow.

Here is where we see the cause of such a drastic fall from that place of union and ecstasy.

They fell for it. They ate from the tree of the knowledge of good and evil, and the human race fell into the pit of sin and separation from God.

Their true sin, I believe, was not only disobedience but also distrust in who they were, which is actually distrust one by whom they were created.

It is evident from the very first moment of their Fall, that guilt, shame, and unbelief had flooded their hearts.

They instantly became ashamed of their nakedness. They hid themselves from the Lord because they feared His punishment.[62] Interestingly, it was not because they had sinned, but because they were naked.

See the instant change in the nature of humankind toward God. They no longer loved Him, but feared Him.

I believe that this Fall did not exactly happen per se when they ate from the tree. What I mean is that disobedience can only spring from an already fallen condition, in the same way that obedience can only spring from faith:

...submission to Him which springs from faith.... [63]

...submission to Him, which is the product of faith. [64]

I believe that they fell the moment they believed that they needed, and became dependent upon, something other than the Lord to sustain or produce their Godlikeness.

This is where religion will always tempt a believer. It tells you that something else is needed to produce a condition of God-likeness other than childlike faith.

The tree itself was not an evil tree, nor was it to blame for Adam's fall; God created it and it was good. This tells us that even good things, when trusted in to produce godliness and right standing with God, can become idols of self-works.

Religion always tells us that we need to do something else to be like God; when in fact we are already like Him! As Christians, we are lifted again to Godlikeness through Christ's work on the cross; it is imparted to us through childlike faith and trust in what He has done.

A childlike response to the work of Christ is all that God requires of us or will accept from us. He just wants us to be awed by Christ's sacrifice!

+ DISOBEDIENCE and Distrust

We see here that the whole problem lies in distrust, not just disobedience. Disobedience is a symptom of the disease of distrust.

The human race fell from that place of absolute pleasure and ecstasy because of distrust. But God in His infinite mercy had a plan—a Lamb who was slain before the foundation of the world.

> ...*the lamb who was slaughtered before the creation of the world.*[65]

Even in that earliest moment of history, to cover the nakedness and shame, we see that the Gospel was preached to Adam and Eve when God Himself killed the animals and clothed them with the skins.

This very first death in the history of creation, the death of the animals that God clothed Adam and Eve with, was a vivid foreshadowing of Christ!

God was preaching to them the Gospel—that Christ's death is the cure for fallen humanity.

> These coats of skin had a significance. The beasts whose skins they were, must be slain; slain before their eyes to show them what death is. And probably 'tis supposed they were slain for sacrifice, to typify the great sacrifice which in the latter end of the world should be offered once for all. Thus the first thing that died was a sacrifice, or Christ in a figure.[66]

The wonderful news of the Gospel is that Christ, through His death, has lifted the curse from humanity.

How glorious a God we have, who does not leave us in this wretched condition but makes a way back into the divine ecstasy of Eden.

> Let our hearts gratefully remember the former loving kindnesses of the Lord: we were sadly

low, sorely distressed, and completely past hope, but when Jehovah appeared he did not merely lift us out of despondency, he raised us into wondering happiness. The Lord who alone turns our captivity does nothing by halves: those whom he saves from hell he brings to heaven. He turns exile into ecstasy, and banishment into bliss.[67]

The first Adam opened the door to sin; the Last Adam (Christ) has opened the door to righteousness.

The ecstasy of salvation that was once lost, has now been recovered—in Christ!

Christ has forever reopened to us the entrance into the Garden of Eden through the torn veil of His flesh.

> *Having therefore, brethren, boldness in the entering into the Holiest by the blood of Jesus, which (entrance into) He inaugurated for us, a road freshly-slain and living, through the veil, namely, His flesh.*[68]

We have entered into union by the way that Christ has paved in blood.

Somehow, miraculously and graciously, we have been placed back into the Garden and grafted into the Tree of Life.

We have been planted together in Christ's death, burial, and resurrection. When He died, we died. When Christ was crucified, our fallenness was crucified and our union with God restored.

> *...if we were planted into the garden of His death*

surely we shall be planted into the garden of His
resurrected life. [69]

It will take eternity to reveal to us the fullness of this mystery, but the simple truth of the Gospel is that we were crucified with Christ, and we now get to enjoy a new life.

What was lost in the Fall was the pleasure of being connected to the Lord; the joy of being one with Him. When man fell, he fell into a separated existence apart from God—an anti-life void of innocence.

But the Gospel declares to us that Christ came and made Himself one with us by taking upon Himself humanity and all its frailties.

He was incarnated and crucified to remove the curse of the Fall.

Through our death with Christ, we have been placed back into the Garden of ecstasy and back into the joys of divine union.

This is the ecstasy that the Gospel announces. It declares your new reality of mystical oneness with Christ.

The Gospel announces the glad tidings—the way out of our fallen condition. It leads us in the instant exodus from the land of sin.

The Gospel offers a new life, in a new land, free from sin and filled with joy and ecstasy!

> *So what do we do? Keep on sinning so God can keep on forgiving? I should hope not! If we've left the country where sin is sovereign, how can we still live in our old house there? Or didn't you realize we packed up and left there for good?*

That is what happened in baptism. When we went under the water, we left the old country of sin behind; when we came up out of the water, we entered into the new country of grace—a new life in a new land! [70]

YOUR NOTES=

This space is provided for you to record your personal insights and thoughts regarding what you have read so far.

_____

_____

_____

_____

_____

_____

_____

_____

_____

_____

_____

_____

05

CHAPTER 5

+ NEW CREATION REALITIES

At the first sip of the Good News, we come face to face with the realities and limitless possibilities of the New Creation.

A Christian is altogether new and enjoys a joy-filled life in a new world. Christians are set free not only from sin and its effects, but are also set free from themselves!

This is how the Distilled Bible describes our new existence:

> I consider myself as having died and now I am enjoying a second existence which is simply Jesus using my body. [71]

The realm people enter then, when they become Christians, is a realm that is no longer merely human. They are lifted out of their corrupted condition and into a divine one. They are raised into the humanity that God had in mind when He created us—humanity in His image!

No longer under the dominion of the cruel ruler sin, we discover the intended, incorruptible, incomparable existence of man.

The Gospel gives us a life that is no longer stuck in the orbit of moral law with the inevitable failure of keeping it through our own willpower. We Christians are now free to explore a new world of endless happiness and holiness.

The Gospel declares that we are new creatures!

There are two Greek words used in the New Testament for the word *new*. The first is *neos*,[72] which means "new with respect to time." *Neos* new, is new of the same kind and of the same quality.

The second Greek word, which I will expound on in this section, is *kainos*. *Kainos* is one of my absolute favorite words in the New Testament.

The definition of *kainos* is "new as to form or quality, of a different nature from what is contrasted as old."[73]

A great explanation of *kainos* is that it is new in kind and in contrast to what previously existed, so that it takes its place.

If something is *kainos*, it is superior to what it succeeds.

Without a doubt, one of my most cherished verses in Scripture where *kainos* is used is in Second Corinthians 5:17.

Here is the first half of this Scripture from several different translations:

So that, assuming that anyone is in Christ, he is a new creation in quality.[74]

Therefore, if anyone is in union with Christ, he is a new being.[75]

For if a man is in Christ he becomes a new person altogether.[76]

When anyone is united to Christ, there is a new world.[77]

We are not the same distorted and corrupted humans we once were, subject to the chains of sin and death.

We are new. We are *kainos new!*

We are new in quality and in kind, and superior to what we were in our fallen state.

The Scripture goes on to say, in the next part of that verse, that not only are we new creations, but that the old being or person we were before we came to Christ, has been made extinct.

His old being has passed away.[78]

His old life has disappeared, everything has become new about him.[79]

The past is finished and gone, everything has become fresh and new.[80]

The old order has gone, and a new order has already begun.[81]

The old order is gone and everything is *new!*

The Greek word here for old is *arkhayos*, which is defined as "the original, primeval,"[82] or "archaic."[83] How amazing! Christ and His cross have destroyed the original and corrupted humanity and have created us anew in Him.

> Numerous popular explanations of Paul's doctrine of the Christian life argue, or assume, that the Apostle distinguishes with these phrases two parts or natures of a person. Following this misguided thinking is the debate as to whether the "old nature" is replaced by the "new" nature' at conversion, or whether the "new nature" is added to the old.
>
> The interpretation that **ho palaios anthropos** and **ho kainos anthropos** refer to parts is wrong and misleading. These terms rather designate the complete person viewed in the corporate whole to which he or she belongs. Thus these terms are better translated as "old person" and "new person"…The translation "old self" and "new self" is too individualistic, since the idea certainly means the individual Christian (see Rom 6:6), but is much more than merely individual.
>
> The "old person" is not just the sin nature, which was judged at the cross and to which is added a "new person". The "old person" is what believers were "in Adam" (in the old era). The "old" points to everything connected with the fall of humanity and with the subjection to the distress and death of a transitory life, separated from God.

The "new person" is what believers are "in Christ" (in the new era). Paul directs us to the completely new, to the salvation and healing that believers receive when they are crucified with Christ and raised with him.[84]

Everything that we were "in Adam" has been shattered and destroyed! We have been completely disconnected from the Fall of humanity and its curse, which is separation from God, and have entered into a new world altogether.

When we came to Christ, we entered into a new era—the era of Christ the Last Adam. This change is not just a change in the nature of humankind; it encompasses far more. It is a change in the corporate whole to which we belong.

In this new era, a *kainos* era, a whole new reality and dimension opens to us. I call it the *kainos* dimension. We are not new creatures still under the curse and Fall of man. We are in a new, divinely-lifted condition.

It's a whole new world!

You may ask, "But aren't we supposed to 'put off' the old man?"

Colossians actually says:

> *Seeing that you have put off the old man with his deeds; and have put on the new man.*[85]

The apostle Paul here is giving the Colossian church their death certificate, leaving no room in the new life for their former evil and sinful behaviors.

The words *put off* and *put on* in this Scripture come from the Greek words *ekduo* and *enduo* meaning "to sink out of, and sink into."[86]

We have sunk out of the old man and have sunk into the new!

I call it the "second fall."

Just as the human race through Adam fell into sin, so we have *fallen* and *sunk into* grace through Christ. Consequently, this fall into grace has a far more encompassing effect than the fall into sin.

> *Adam prefigured the One to come, but the gift itself considerably outweighed the fall...the results of the gift also outweigh the results of the one man's sin.*[87]

In our union with Christ, we have entered into a new existence in a new world of endless bliss. This is the realm and reality believers enjoy as a gift when they drink freely of the New Covenant. Not only were our sinful selves and natures crucified, but also we were raised into a new life.

Christ not only set us free from sin but also its effects and its consequences.

> *...My Servant,* [shall] *justify many and make many righteous (upright and in right standing with God), for He shall bear their iniquities and their guilt [with the consequences, says the Lord].*[88]

We should no longer be limited by the curse and Fall of Man.

In the world of the New Creation, the *kainos* world, all things are possible for those who believe. The New Creation world is "The Kingdom of Heaven," which has invaded the earth through the work of Christ.

As a New Creation, you enjoy not just a change in your being; this change also affects everything around you.

If we suppose that this New Creation reality is truly what Paul writes it is, we must acknowledge many glorious truths that are available to us. We must realize that this changes everything! Our eyes have to be opened to the reality that He makes everything new!

> *Behold, I am doing a new thing! Now it springs forth; do you not perceive and know it and will you not give heed to it?*[89]

+ The *NEW* Heart

As Christians, our old heart that was mastered and owned by desires contrary to the nature of God, has been removed by the Christ and replaced with a brand-new heart.

> *...I'll give you a new heart, put a new spirit in you. I'll remove the stone heart from your body and replace it with a heart that's God-willed, not self-willed....*[90]

This new heart that we have is a new *God-willed* heart because it is a *God-filled* heart.

> *...that you may be filled [through all your being] unto all the fullness of God [may have the richest measure of the divine Presence, and become a body wholly filled and flooded with God Himself]!*[91]

Because of this God-flood, the former heart is eclipsed to absolutely nothing more than a memory.

In fact, the rotten old heart is only called upon as a cause for rejoicing that it has disappeared. Like an empty prison cell, it is only remembered by the former resident as a reminder of how fantastic freedom from that cell really is.

The *old heart* can be defined as "everything about us that was contrary to the nature of God." This old heart, that could never please God, has been cut away by Christ Himself.[92]

True circumcision is of the heart. We Christians have been heart-circumcised!

Here are some translation treasures from Romans 2:28-29:

> *For the true Jew is not the man who is outwardly a Jew, and true circumcision is not that which is outward and bodily. But the true Jew is one inwardly, and true circumcision is heart-circumcision—not literal, but spiritual. Such a man receives praise not from men, but from God.*[93]

> *He is the Jew who is so in his secret soul; and his is the true circumcision—that of the heart, consisting in this Spirit's presence, not in observance of the written letter. Men may have no praise to bestow on such a man—God has.*[94]

> *The word "Jew" properly means "praiseworthy;" and so the true Jew, the man who is truly praiseworthy, is he whose heart is pure in God's sight, whose circumcision is not literal but spiritual—the circumcision of the heart, as the prophets called it.*[95]

> *...the real circumcision is a thing of the heart. It is*

a spiritual thing, not conformity to any set of rules and regulations.[96]

...true circumcision is achieved in the heart.[97]

The Lord is not trying to fix the old heart—He has removed it! Amazingly, He does not stop there but places inside of each believer a *new* heart.

In Adam Clarke's words, the Lord goes on to say:

> I will change the whole of your infected nature; and give you new appetites, new passions....
>
> I will entirely remove this heart: it is opposite to that which I have promised you; you cannot have the new heart and the old heart at the same time.[98]

You cannot have the old and new at the same time; they are opposite of each other and have contrary desires.

But a true Christian has only a heart that is by nature completely new. This heart has new passions and emotions. These are the emotions of the Spirit.

The new heart frolics in the presence of God; for it has been made the dwelling place of the Eternal! The new heart is a holy heart, with only holy thoughts and desires.

There is nothing evil in the heart of the believer! Only Heaven's goodness can dwell within it.

> *...only goodness, mercy, and unfailing love shall follow me all the days of my life...[99]*

+ The *GLORIFIED* Emotions

I believe that holy emotions are one of the greatest portals that God uses to invade the world.

In fact, the Scripture says that even faith is evidenced by love, *"...the only essential condition being a faith which gives evidence of its vital power by love."*[100]

Now I know that love is not merely an emotion, but I dare anyone to show me an emotionless love.

Love, I believe, is *divine* emotion.

It is a *God* emotion!

Emotions like love and joy are not normal. They are simply not human inventions. Humankind was hardwired with God-given emotions, and in spite of contrary belief, they are not the ill effect of the Fall. The Lord created our emotions to be strong and intense because He desires us to love Him strongly and intensely.

Let me just say that God hates depression! It is opposite of His nature, and He would never leave the child of God in its grip.

Happy are the people of God![101]

The reason most Christians live on an emotional rollercoaster is because they have not realized their union with Christ. They don't realize that the change in our nature goes that deep.

Emotions submit to the master of the house. If sin is your master, your emotions are under sin's rule. So the question is: Who do you believe to be your master?

Are you a sinner?

Or are you a saint?

If you are a believer and you are having trouble answering these questions, let me quickly help you.

You are a saint!

Your Master is Christ, not sin.

The evil that fills the hearts of unbelievers hijacks their emotions and employs them for its purposes.

But if Christ is the Master of the house, your emotions will bow to Him whom they were created for and will be glorified by Him.

When you become Christ's, you become the recipient of His emotions and His desires. The desires of the Spirit become yours.

It's very funny—I often hear people saying, *"If it is the Lord's desire I'll do it."*

Let's just make it really easy.

If you are a born-again child of God and you have a desire to do something for the Kingdom...do it! He is the One who produces that desire in your heart. It is the Spirit's emotions that are now running through you.

A Christian, whose heart is filled no longer with evil but with rivers of love, finds his emotions given over to that perfect love and carried wherever its rivers take him.

Our emotions are now used to worship Him. We worship Him with laughter, joy, and emotional affections.

> *...When the righteous see God in action they'll laugh, they'll sing, they'll laugh and sing for joy.*[102]

As newly created beings, we are now able to love Him with our whole heart, soul, mind, and strength. Our emotions are obviously included somewhere within this list.

One thing that I've observed about emotions is that they are wonderful outward signs of inward possession.

In fact, love, a holy emotion, is how we are known to be His. Our affections for the Lord and one another are defining marks of Christianity.

The emotions and desires of the Spirit aren't something you can strive for. Holy emotions should come naturally to a believer. When you are overmastered by love, love bursts out of you. When you are jam-packed with joy unspeakable, joy flows like an unstoppable river.

When you are filled with the nature of the Prince of Peace, peace comes naturally. In fact, when the Savior possesses you, even your salvation becomes more effortless than breathing!

This is the sweet reality of the Christian life. It is an existence that is completely possessed by the presence and goodness of God, and expressed by glorified emotions.

+ The *GLORIFIED* Body

Without a doubt, most Christians view the body as a vile and evil entity that must be subdued through much effort. This is not the reality that Christ gives us in His infinite love and with His perfect sacrifice.

The body is not in and of itself evil at all. It is a creation and master work of art by the Master of Holiness, created to carry the life of the Spirit. It is not sinful, but it is used as the instrument of sin.[103] Sin uses the body to carry out its evil acts.

Following the idea that the body is evil is the belief that Christians will never be free from sin until they die and are released from their bodies.

Do you see how wild that idea is? Death, which is the effect of sin, is supposed to free you from sin (see Rom. 8:2).

If death delivers us from what Christ could not, then death, not Christ, becomes our savior!

> ...how positively do some hold out death as the complete deliverer from all corruption, and the final destroyer of sin, as if it were revealed in every page of the Bible! Whereas, there is not one passage in the sacred volume that says any such thing. Were this true, then death, far from being the last enemy, would be the last and best friend, and the greatest of all deliverers: for if the last remains of all the indwelling sin of all believers is to be destroyed by death, (and a fearful mass this will make,) then death, that removes it, must be the highest benefactor of mankind. The truth is, he is neither the cause nor the means of its destruction. It is the blood of Jesus alone that cleanseth from all unrighteousness.[104]

Our bodies have been cleansed and glorified. As Christians, our members now are members of righteousness. Our bodies are carriers of holiness.

The body is designed, like our emotions, to be subservient to whoever its master is. It is under the dominion of whoever owns it, whether it is darkness or light, sinfulness or righteousness, life or death. When owned by darkness, it is enslaved to its purposes. But when owned by Christ, the body is gloriously enslaved to love and to be loved by Him!

The body of the Christian is employed to express and demonstrate the radical love of Christ and to be put on display for all to see the divine life flowing through it. It is given totally over to His life and His righteousness. The ones whose bodies are owned by Christ have His very eternal life flowing through their veins!

The product of sin is death, but God's gift to us is eternal life. This eternal life doesn't start when you die; it started when you believed in Christ.

This is why we can believe and trust in Christ's sacrifice to be perfectly sufficient for divine health all of our lives.

My wife, Stephanie, has been a wonderful demonstration not only of supernatural healing but also of divine health.

About seven years ago, while we were ministering in a church in rural Illinois, Stephanie had a weird sensation in her body. She said she felt her whole body going numb. I thought this was wonderful, thinking it might be some sort of ecstasy coming upon her, but she said, "No, it's not the good kind of numb." I knew then that something was very wrong.

I quickly drove her to the hospital and within a matter of minutes Stephanie had become completely paralyzed. After weeks of many nasty tests and needles, the doctors told us that she had Guillian-Barre Syndrome. She spent almost two months paralyzed in the hospital.

They gave us such gloomy and negative reports. They told us that Stephanie would never be able to walk normally again. If she did walk, she would have to use a cane or a walker, as they said most people never make a full recovery. They told us that her immune system had been severely weakened and that she could not go to foreign countries or travel for ministry anymore.

I hated hearing these things; I knew it wasn't the truth. We both knew that Jesus had something better for us than that.

I decided to joyfully ignore the doctors' orders of "not having too much excitement" in Stephanie's hospital room, and I gathered everyone I knew who loved Jesus and believed that this was not our portion.

We went in and just worshiped and enjoyed Jesus and had fun. We felt Jesus' presence so sweet and intense there and every time we worshiped, without fail, Stephanie's heart monitor would go off the charts! Nonstop melodies of life were flooding her room.

While Stephanie slept, I would sing silly songs to her and serenade her.

Finally the syndrome was not progressing anymore, and they decided to send Stephanie home; yet, she was still paralyzed. There was nothing more they could do for her. Her best hope was to go to physical therapy every day, build up her muscle mass, and learn to walk again.

One day while Stephanie was alone and really wanting to go to the restroom by herself, without someone carrying her or wheeling her in, she heard the Lord say to her, "Get up and go!"

So she did.

She stood up for the first time in months. She was healed!

Within a few days, she had regained all of her strength and had become perfectly healthy!

She had not only fully recovered and supernaturally regained her muscle mass without one day of physical therapy, but she had a glow and a freshness on her body. The only way to describe it is if you can imagine what someone looks like when he or she has been raised from the dead. It's a brightness that can be seen on someone's physical body.

Stephanie personally wheeled her wheelchair into the hospital, skipping and dancing, and told them that she would never need it again.

Since then, about seven years now, Stephanie has not been sick at all.

I don't mean the syndrome—I mean absolutely *no* sickness! Not the flu, not a cold, not the sniffles…nothing!

Stephanie is living in divine health.

Since then we have traveled together in nonstop itinerant ministry to countless countries, garbage dumps, leper colonies, and slums all around the world. I have seen her play with some of the dirtiest kids on Earth in the garbage dumps of Asia and unreservedly kiss lepers in India.

Every year we go on an "Around-the-World Garbage Dump Tour" circling the globe, loving the poor; and there is never even a trace of sickness in Stephanie.

Stephanie is truly a sign and wonder of a glorified body. Life is her inheritance that Jesus paid for.

When in union with Christ, life and not death is the ruling factor in our lives. Sickness and disease can no longer reign in a body owned by life—Christ has purchased us.

Our claim to healing and health is that we belong to Christ and to His righteousness, and this produces life in our bodies. Our spirits, souls, and even our bodies are subject to newness. We have been *"recreated in Christ Jesus."*[105] We are to yield our bodies as though we have been raised from the dead.[106]

Our bodies are now sharing in Christ's life, the same Life that raised Christ's (physical) body from the dead. That same (physical) body resurrecting power is now dwelling inside of us believers. It is part of our new reality as new creations.

Life is our portion.

It is amazing to see that on the day of Christ's resurrection, He was not the only one who was raised from death.

The power of death over the body was defeated!

> *The tombs were opened and many bodies of the saints who had fallen asleep in death were raised [to life]; and coming out of the tombs after His resurrection, they went into the holy city and appeared to many people.*[107]

Mortality had been *"drunk down by God."*[108]

Even our bodies are affected by our new condition of union with Christ. We are sharing Christ's glorification!

> *...and those whom He justified, He also glorified [raising them to a heavenly dignity and condition or state of being].*[109]

The Christian body is the carrier of Christ Himself!

+ All Get UPGRADED

Possibly one roadblock that keeps us from actually experiencing and enjoying this wonderful reality that I have been describing, is that we tend to compartmentalize and separate the things concerning our salvation.

Sort of like a child, who instead of waking up Christmas morning, running down the stairs, diving into the presents like a wild beast, and tearing open everything that has paper and a bow, he calmly sorts each present out one by one, taking all day to open his gifts.

Sadly though, in reality it takes most of a lifetime to realize the gifts of Heaven, to open and to enjoy them. Even then, many are still left unopened under the tree.

We tend to separate each gift from God and put them into little boxes, all nice and neat. It is a silly thought, but this is the norm for most Christian lives.

We say, "I'm saved, but now I need the infilling of the Holy Ghost."

Truthfully, when Christ came into our hearts, so came the Spirit and the Father and all the fullness of the Godhead.[110]

These are inseparable!

And when the Holy Spirit came into our hearts He came bearing wonderful gifts. And truly the most wonderful of these is sanctification and holiness.

Let me just say that the initial evidence of the infilling of the Holy Spirit is—*holiness!*

He is the *Holy* Spirit!

We shouldn't compartmentalize everything, making salvation process-based. When someone becomes a believer, we should give that person the whole package, not just a drink, and lead him or her to the rivers of salvation.

Or, sometimes what happens is we try to tier our salvation experience like a frequent flyer program. The longer we fly, the more ladders we climb; the more religious dues we pay, the more upgrades we get.

What we have then is a multitiered Christianity, with some holier than others!

Sanctification, holiness, and every other good thing, though being works of Christ, available freely once and for all at the moment of salvation, then become progressive works based not on the efforts of Christ but ours—on how long and how hard we've worked for them.

What we literally have then, are some people who are "holier than thou." This is obviously not the Gospel! Though most wouldn't put this as candidly as I do, this is where these programs and separations lead.

The true Gospel is when Christ gave Himself to us and for us, He did it unreservedly. He opened wide the doors of Heaven and all its wonders and gifts for all who will believe.

I say we drink our fill!

I say we drink it all!

I say we drink till our hearts are fat and bursting with God's glories, and then let's drink some more!

Included in this unlocked storehouse of Heaven are the gifts of sanctification and holiness: being completely set apart for His pleasure.

Our hearts were once and for all mastered at the instant the truth of the Gospel penetrated them and we believed.

With receiving Christ we receive all that He is.

Christ, of course, is the infilling.

He is Joy.

He is Love.

He is our righteousness.

He is our sanctification![111]

The truth is, all get upgraded, regardless of their Christian frequent flyer status. No matter how long we've been Christians or been in the Master's vineyard, we all get the same pay—which is everything!

The Master is very generous! We should never reject or be envious of His generosity.[112]

All of us who are believers are lifted from the pit of sinfulness and self-possession into the glorious and heavenly perfections of Christ.

The gift is given freely to all, without reservation. That all-inclusive, satisfying gift is Christ!

YOUR NOTES=

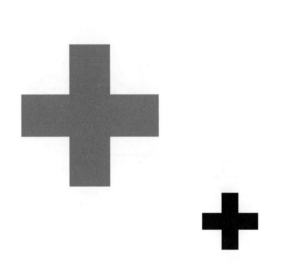

06

+ IT'S A SCANDAL!

When I first became a believer, many people told me that God's way is hard, that Christianity is a struggle, and many stumbling blocks lie in the way.

But in fact, through devouring the Scriptures and through feasting upon its realities, I have come to realize that the true stumbling block is the *ease* of the Gospel.

That's right, the ease!

The dependent and trusting do not stumble at this rock. To them this rock bursts with living water. To those who are believers, this rock oozes pure honey.[113]

Those who stumble at this block demand salvation by their own achievements. It trips only those who are seeking a way other than the cross and the Christ.

Most of us have been in this place or are in this place because we are simply unaware of the Gospel's goodness. We have never been told what amazing freedom is offered to us.

My hope is that after reading this book, you will fall into the effortlessness of believing and become possessed by the joys of childlike trust.

The stumbling block that I'm talking about is mainly the preaching of instantaneous righteousness and union through Christ's cross. It is the offence of the cross.

> *We preach Christ (the Messiah) crucified, [preaching which] to the Jews is a **scandal** and an offensive **stumbling block** [that springs a snare or trap]....*[114]

The word for "stumbling block" is *skandalon* in Greek. It is where we get the transliterated word *scandal*.

It is also defined as, "a trap stick, offence or thing that offends."

The cross is the divine scandal!

Why is it a scandal and a trap stick?

Here is Thayer's definition of the word: "applied to Christ, whose person and career were so contrary to the expectations of the Jews concerning the Messiah that they rejected him and by their obstinacy made a shipwreck of their salvation."[115]

It is a scandal because in the crucifixion of Christ we see God's way of salvation for humankind.

We see that man, with his best efforts, could never pay the cost required, not only for sin but also of love.

He did not merely punish sin, but found a way to display His love for us through His sufferings. This is the genius of the sacrifice of Christ.

> Punishment would be partial in comparison with this. It would evidence but one aspect of God's being. But the humiliation, sufferings, and death of the Son of God, prompted by infinite love, represent and satisfy the total perfection of God.[116]

The scandal is that though your sin was great, God's love was greater. You might conclude that you should bring an offering for your acceptance with God, yet Christ has beaten you to it. That's the scandal.

It is a scandal of love.

We couldn't provide a sacrifice, so God provided one for Himself—in Christ. We couldn't climb to Heaven, so Heaven came to us—in Christ. In Christ, we see the grand display of the heavens invading the earth.

This scandal is designed to make you blush. Its intention is to make every cell in your body scream with thanksgiving and joyful praise!

+ HE PROVIDED The Sacrifice

In Genesis chapter 22, there is a great parable of this divine scandal. It is a familiar story to most Christians, but allow the Holy Ghost to shed some new light upon this portion of Scripture.

We read that Abraham is told to offer his son Isaac as a sacrifice to God. Remember, this is the same Isaac who was promised to Abraham and was supernaturally conceived.

The first clue we receive here that this is more than a test of Abraham's faith is when Abraham, by divine revelation, says to his servant, "I and my son Isaac will go and worship then come back." [117]

How did Abraham know that he and Isaac would return again, when Abraham was commanded to sacrifice Isaac?

The writer of Hebrews brilliantly reveals the mystery here. In Hebrews chapter 11, it says that *"By faith Abraham...offered up Isaac... Accounting that God was able to raise him up, even from the dead...in a figure."*[118]

The word *figure* is *parabole* in Greek.[119]

A parable!

The story of Abraham offering up Isaac is a parable of Christ's sacrifice!

It is an earthly story with a heavenly meaning.

The parable goes on and Isaac says to his father: "Behold the fire and the wood: but where is the lamb...? And Abraham said, My son, God will provide Himself a lamb..."[120]

...the patriarch spoke prophetically, and referred to that Lamb of God which he had provided for himself, who in the fullness of time should take away the sin of the world, and whom Isaac was a most expressive type. All the other lambs which had been offered from the foundation of the world had been such as Men chose and Men offered; but This was the Lamb which God had provided—emphatically, The Lamb of God.[121]

The story here is not one of the offering of Abraham, but it is a story of the offering of God.

The Message Bible says, *"But the story we're given is a God-story, not an Abraham-story."* [122]

It is a peek into the story of redemption, where God would provide the Lamb.

We read on and see that just as Abraham was about to slay his only son, whom he loved, the angel of the Lord (the Lord Jesus Christ Himself) said, *"Do not lay a hand on the boy."*

Abraham lifted up his eyes and saw a ram caught in the thicket. He lifted his eyes to Heaven and saw, in a prophetic parable, the Lamb of God crowned with thorns.

Then Abraham called the name of that place "Jehovah-Jireh," literally, *"the place where the Lord will provide."*

The Scripture goes on to say, *"On this mountain the provision of the Lord shall be seen."*

> From this it appears that the sacrifice offered by Abraham was understood to be a representative one, and a tradition was kept up that Jehovah should be seen in a sacrificial way on this mount.[123]

It is more than probable that this is the very same mount where Christ was crucified.

Abraham was told to go to sacrifice his son in the mountains of

Moriah. The Lord said that He would show him exactly which mountain.

> The land of Moriah—this is supposed to mean all the mountains of Jerusalem…As Mount Calvary is the highest ground to the west, and the mount of the temple is the lowest of the mounts, Mr. Mann conjectures that it was upon this mount Abraham offered up Isaac, which is well known to be the same mount on which our blessed Lord was crucified.[124]

Though religion would have us believe this is a story of the self-sacrifice of Abraham that demands our following, it is actually a picture of the self-sacrifice of Christ. It is the ram caught in the thicket, the substitute, which is the star in this play!

It is a divine parable of God's provision of the Lamb.

This is a scandalizing look at what God requires of us. He does not require us to lay our promises upon the altar—but the Promised One upon the altar.

+ HE BORE Our Crosses

Much is spoken about sacrifice in modern Christianity. Sadly, it rarely concerns Christ's sacrifice upon the cross.

The view of Christ for many is that He was a template after whom we should order our lives. They view His work on the cross as their highest example, to which they should follow.

Many see Him as a formula, or a guide to teach them how to be a miracle worker, be a good leader, and live a moral life.

Though Jesus was all of these, He never wanted us to view Him exclusively in this way.

Numerous believers see Christ merely as the doorway and not the destination. We are not only to know Jesus the Messiah as our example, but as our substitute!

Yes, of course He is the perfect example of holy living, but His purpose was not to show us how to live, but to live it out for us—in us and through us.

He didn't come to show us how *not to sin*, He came to *break sin's power* over us. He came to destroy the rule of sin that possessed us. Absorbing the spirit of sin upon Himself and crucifying it accomplished this once and for all.

Everything Jesus said and did in His life, His miracles, His teachings, and His parables should be seen in light of His death. His death on the cross wasn't just a part of His purpose—it was His purpose!

> The death of Jesus on the cross was the culmination of His saving work and the crowning glory of his Messianic vocation.[125]

Jesus was born to die; He was born to give His life as a substitutionary offering.

Though Jesus never demands this same sacrifice from us, what He does demand is that we drink from His—drink the cup of *His* sacrifice.

Christianity is about *Christ!*

It's all about *Christ's cross.*

Jesus said, "Whoever wants to come after Me, let him deny

himself, take up his cross, and follow Me" (see Matt. 16:24).

This seems to be one of the most twisted and misunderstood verses in the Bible. To most people, this verse seems more like another burden to bear, rather than a burden lifted, which is its intended meaning.

Jesus said first, "Follow Me."

Where was He going?

He was going to Jerusalem to be crucified and to pay the ransom for all humankind, to lift the burden of sin from humanity.

This Scripture is not a call for the self-sacrifice of the disciples or the believer but a call to follow and trust in Christ and His work that He was about to accomplish on the cross.

He had just revealed this to His disciples in the previous verses. And of course, good ol' Peter rebuked Jesus for saying such crazy things.

This "Crucified Messiah" did not fit into Peter's grid. The same could be said about many Christians today.

In the most practical sense, Jesus was saying to His disciples, "Hey guys, we got some rough times ahead. I'm gonna be killed pretty soon but it will be OK. You boys better stick with Me; I know what I'm doing. Don't go running off on your own and getting yourselves into trouble. Just trust Me!"

Though circumstances may come, we must continue to trust in Jesus because it's all going to work out for our good.

Are you saying that the Christian life is all peaches and cream?

Well, in a sense, yes!

It is Christ who bore our burdens, and continues to bear them and us to Himself. In our trying and hard times, we are to rejoice even more, knowing that Christ has everything sovereignly in His hands.

I'm not saying that hard times don't come; I'm simply saying that you can have supernatural joy in the midst of them. In the eternal sense, this verse means that we are to follow after Christ's sacrifice, not mimic it, but trust in it alone for our salvation and sustainment.

This verse in Matthew 16 in no way implies that believers have anything to do with the removal of sin from their lives by carrying their own cross.

Here is a simple question: *Whose cross was Jesus carrying?*

His own?

No way!

When Christ was hanging naked and mutilated on the tree of Calvary, it was not for His own crimes, but ours. He was murdered! He was innocent of all evil.

He was our scapegoat—the substitution for all of humanity.

He was not carrying His cross; He was carrying our crosses!

Winnie Banov, who is like a mother to me, once told me a story of how she made several crosses out of toothpicks and handed them out during one of her teachings to illustrate how light our crosses are, if indeed we demand to have our own.

Hilarious!

The truth is that the believer's cross is even lighter still, lighter than a toothpick!

This sounds strange I know, but this is the whole point of Christianity and salvation. Christ carried our cross and paid the price that we could not.

This is the glorious liberty that Christ has given to us.

The reason He wants us to follow Him to the cross is to show us firsthand where our slavery to sin ended. We follow Him to Calvary so we can see with our own eyes and examine for ourselves our wretchedness hung upon the tree.

In these Scriptures, Christ is inviting us to approach Him not with fists full of deeds but with empty hands, declaring our dependence and need for a Savior.

It is an invitation to trade our unbearable burden for His, which is easy; to take upon us His yoke, which is light.[126]

We must have His yoke and He must bear ours because we cannot bear our own. We must let Him wash our feet and serve us with His sacrifice even though it may confuse everything we ever thought about Christ; unless we let Him do this, we can have no part with Him.[127]

He commands us to "deny self"—this word here actually means "to forget and lose sight of self."[128]

The sense here in this Scripture is not self-sacrifice in the way that most would see it. It actually is a call to deny any heavenly advancement through self-achievement. It means that salvation or any of its benefits cannot be owed or due to ourselves!

Young's Literal Translation says, *"…let him disown himself."*[129]

And *"…he must give up all rights to himself,"* says the Phillips translation.[130]

We do not own ourselves anymore! As Christians, we are possessed by Christ.

We have joyfully given up all of our rights to a sinful, independent existence and have been enraptured in mystical union and dependence upon Christ.

This is not a lifelong process; how can it be? When we came to Christ, we were offered such beauty and blessing that we instantly lost sight of anything else.

This is the true meaning of denying ourselves—we are no longer in charge, even of our salvation! Come life, come death, persecution or promotion, we are not our own. We are blissfully and eternally His! Losing the rights to ourselves, we are totally given over to trusting Him.

If you feel that you have had it wrong all this time and are still trying to deny yourself, I have a simple solution. Look at Christ's cross and the blessings offered because of it, and simply lose sight of your own achievements—simply lose sight of *self*.

Let *self* be eclipsed by the glory of the cross.

You might be asking: *Aren't we supposed to work out our own salvation with fear and trembling?*

Read that verse from the A.S. Way translation:

> *…work out, with fear and self-distrust, ay, with trembling self-distrust, your own salvation. You have not to do it in your unaided strength: it is God who is all the while supplying the impulse….*[131]

Enlightening, isn't it.

Paul wrote this during his Roman imprisonment awaiting possible death. Knowing that he might never return to his beloved Philippian church, his most generous supporter, he lovingly tells them that they must not rely upon him any longer but they must trust in the impulse of God within them.

The apostle was essentially teaching them to drink from the Source of salvation, and not just be the messengers of it.

The sense of the Scripture is not working out our salvation in our own strength, but in fact, it is the opposite. It is that we should trust none but God alone, who is giving us the strength and the impulse for our salvation. We should approach our salvation with trembling *self-distrust*, resting solely in God's wondrous ability.

If we miss the meaning of these simple Scriptures, we are in danger of placing the emphasis upon ourselves instead of on *Christ.*

For we are *"partakers of Christ's salvation,"*[32] as the Amplified Bible puts it.

Christ is our substitute; His sacrifice should not, and indeed cannot, be followed. I'm not talking about giving our lives in martyrdom for the Gospel; I'm talking about attempting to pay a price that only He was anointed to pay.

He was the Anointed One; He was the only One ordained to give His life as an offering for sin, to make man righteous before God. It was His place to be offered to God as a pure, spotless Lamb, One who would take away the sin of the world.

And this He did. He did offer that sacrifice and did take away our sin. We, who are His, are free from the power and rule of sin.

We lost our wretched sinful lives and gained ones that are filled with heavenly pleasure. We lost the world of sin and gained one filled with righteousness.

We are not sinners—we are saints!

Now, as believers, we follow Christ not because we want to be like Him, but because we *are* like Him!

We love Him because He first loved us. He is the Author and Finisher of our faith. It always starts and ends with Christ. The middle is where most get off track, but let me tell you an open secret—He is the middle also!

The common purpose, for most Christians, for daily self-denial and sacrifice, is the belief that by this they will become more righteous. This, though commonly advocated, is not how true righteousness is attained.

I understand this may shock many.

I agree it is shocking.

It is shockingly good!

+ HIS WAY of Righteousness

I saw the connection between the "righteousness from God" and the statement that "the righteous will live by faith." Then I grasped that the righteousness from God is that righteousness by which through grace and sheer mercy God justifies us through faith. All at once I felt myself to have been born again and to have gone through open gates of paradise itself. The whole of Scripture took on a new meaning, and whereas before the "righteousness from God" had filled me with hate, now it became to me inexpressibly sweet in greater love. This passage of Paul had become to me the very gate to paradise. —Martin Luther[133]

Have you entered into paradise through these same gates?

God's kind of righteousness comes only through faith, and faith placed in something very specific—faith in the substitutionary sacrifice of Christ.

This is the treasure that the apostle Paul penned in Romans, and the prophet Habakkuk hundreds of years before him. It is that the righteous shall live by faith![134]

In the Gospel *"there is revealed the righteousness which has God for its source, the righteousness that springs from faith and leads to faith."* [135]

Most of us Christians know this in principle, and would agree theologically, but *when it comes down to it, most don't know the Lord's way of righteousness, and therefore cannot experience the reality of it.*

Most are striving for something that is simply a gift.

Positionally, most believe that they are holy, but sin still has its grip upon their hearts. The idea of a holy and righteous life is simply that—an idea, not a reality.

This positional theology leaves holiness and union with Christ in some far-off, unattainable place. This is obviously why many aren't living holy and happy lives; they don't believe it is a possibility.

But the Good News declares to us something different! It declares that righteousness is a reality to all who live by faith. In fact, even the word *salvation* carries in it the thought of righteousness. We are saved from sin into holiness.

How can we claim salvation if we are not saved from sin's power?

Don't you think that God had something better in mind for us?

Don't you think that Christianity is something better than a lifelong wrestling match with sin?

Let me just say that there is an enormous difference between morality and righteousness. There are plenty of moral men who don't know God and don't know righteousness.

Even the apostle Paul said in Philippians, referring to his Pharisaic morality, that "according to the righteousness of the Law"[136] he was blameless.

But this was not the righteousness God accepted!

Here is Philippians 3:8-9 from the A.S. Way translation:

> *For His sake I have let all that wealth of mine be confiscated: I count it but as refuse, so I may but gain Messiah, may be found in union with Him, possessing no self-won righteousness—such as is supposed to some through observance of the Mosaic Law—but that alone which is won through faith in Messiah, the righteousness whose source is God, whose foundation is faith.*[137]

What is described in this Scripture is true righteousness. Its source is God and its foundation is faith. This true righteousness is not positional but personal.

It is the person of Jesus Christ who is our righteousness and our sanctification.[138] It is real and has a real and eternal effect upon our souls.

True righteousness is a righteousness bestowed upon humanity as a divine gift of His grace, drunk down by faith, and evidenced by love.

No sacrifice of man can manufacture this kind of righteousness. Merely following Christ's example cannot produce this.

Only by faith in the work of Calvary, by being made one with Him who is righteousness, can we see this manifest.

+ PERFECT Salvation

Let's explore the idea of perfect salvation that runs through the veins of this glorious Gospel.

Perfection is flowing from the heart of God Himself, for He is perfect. Absolutely everything about Him and His nature is perfect. Everything that He does is perfect.

We are to "be perfect, even as our Father which is in heaven is perfect."[139]

When Christ tells us to *be perfect,* it should not be a shock. Well, maybe it should, but He is allowed to shock us here and there. But in light of His goodness, nothing less should be expected.

This perfection that Jesus is telling us to be can mean no less than that we are to be filled with the perfect nature of the Father. Just as He is, so we are privileged to be.

> ...these words of our Lord include both a command and a promise. "Can we be fully saved from sin

in this world?" is an important question, to which this text gives a satisfactory answer: "Ye shall be perfect, as your Father, who is in heaven is perfect." — As in his infinite nature there is no sin, nothing but goodness and love, so in your finite nature there shall dwell no sin....[140]

Christ paid a price for this perfection that is beyond measure, and it should not be in vain.

The body that was prepared for the Son of God, and the blood that poured copiously down His body and spilled upon the ground, was supremely perfect. It is and will forever be perfectly able to secure a divinely flawless salvation for all.

> By means of this perfect sacrifice Christ has introduced a new order...the perfect salvation.[141]

> For by one effectual sacrifice He has provided a perfect salvation for those who believe on Him.[142]

Adam Clarke writes brilliantly:

> This perfection is the restoration of man to the state of holiness from which he fell, by creating him anew in Christ Jesus, and restoring to him that image and likeness of God which he has lost....

> But if man be not perfectly saved from all sin, sin does triumph, and Satan exult, because they have done a mischief that Christ either cannot or will not remove. To say he cannot, would be shocking blasphemy against the infinite power and dignity of the great Creator; to say he will

not, would be equally such against the infinite benevolence and holiness of his nature.[143]

The word *perfect* by definition means "to be complete, lacking nothing from purpose, finished."[144]

Being a Christian means that you are in Christ. We are in perfect union with Him; this is what you and I were created for.

This is Christian perfection—to be one with Christ, who is infinitely perfect. That is our purpose, our finish line, and our completion!

The shocking truth that we discover in the Gospel is that Christ has already run that race for us while we weren't looking, and has won!

Our blissful destiny is to be swallowed up into oceans of *perfect* love. So sweet is His love, that the heart found by this love never needs to look elsewhere. For this heart, sin has lost its flavor and its attraction.

A Christian's biggest temptation should not be sin, but Christ!

In this vast ocean of possessing love, there is no other governing force than the pounding waves of His beauty and His imparted righteousness. Where is darkness when we are staring awestruck into His blinding holiness?

How can evil dwell in the house where celestial goodness holds the keys? How can sin take hold of a heart that is married to another?

Perfection is like treasure people spend all their lives searching for. They sail endlessly on the rough and stormy seas of self-effort and willpower, never knowing that the treasure was in their house the whole time. They never even needed set sail to find what they were looking for. They were finished before they started, and the prize lay right under their noses!

Trusting in the finished work of Christ is the one and only key to unlock perfection. And you need to look no further than Christ in you!

YOUR NOTES=

07

+ TOO GOOD TO BE TRUE?

With these wondrous truths discovered in the Gospel, we are left with the immediate thought that this is too good to be true.

> Can Christianity be this good?

> God's whole way of salvation seems almost too easy!

I ask then, what else should we expect from an intensely loving God?

Shall we demand a harder route, one that requires more sweat and effort on our part? There are many religions taking that difficult road, but none will ever find their way to the prize of salvation.

No, we will only arrive at salvation when we lie down in the green pastures of the work of the cross. Then will we be refreshed and our lives restored by the sweet spring flowing from the side of the Lamb.

+ An *EFFORTLESS* Entry Is Offered

In Numbers chapters 13 and 14, we see this "too good to be true" syndrome's effect upon the children of Israel.

We read that Moses sent out twelve spies to search out the Promised Land. The spies came to a place called *Eschol*, meaning "cluster."[145] There at Eschol, they saw with their own eyes the blessing that was upon the land. They found there a cluster of grapes that took two, fully grown men to carry it on a staff![146] This was the sign of extreme goodness and bounty of the land.

After forty days, they returned to the camp of the Israelites with the news and evidence of the fruit of the Promised Land.

We read that all of the spies, except Joshua and Caleb, gave an evil report. They reported to the Israelite camp, "We are grasshoppers in our own eyes,"[147] speaking of the many enemies in the land and their supposed impossible defeat. We see here that their viewpoint was not from the abilities of their great God, but from their own, since they said "in our own eyes."

Remember, these were the same men who saw the awesome deliverance from Egypt, the greatest superpower on Earth. It is a good point to remember that not only did the children of Israel see the deliverance from Egypt, but they also watched its destruction. After the ten devastating plagues upon the land, the water sources were polluted and the livestock annihilated.

The whole economy was ruined and without an heir to the throne; Egypt was utterly destroyed.

When Caleb heard the unbelieving report that was given, he cried out with absolute faith in his awesome God and said, "Let's go up now and take our land that our God has promised us!"

But again, out spewed unbelief from the mouths of the other spies, as they stirred the people by their unjust description of the Promised Land.

All of Israel went into an uproar of distrust. The people, in a frenzy of unbelief, wanted to choose a new leader who would take them back to Egypt.

Again, remember that these children were not only delivered from the slavery of Egypt, but Egypt was totally destroyed. It was a fantasy of unbelief to think that there was an Egypt to return to! There literally was nothing left in Egypt but ruins of a once-great country.

See how quickly unbelief makes one forget the miracles that God has performed.

At this, Joshua and Caleb ripped their clothes and demanded that they go up and take the land at once. They remembered the deliverance of the Lord and knew that the report of the defeat of Egypt had swiftly swept across the land. Joshua said, "Their defense has departed them."[148]

They pleaded with Israel to be convinced that the Lord was with them, and that their entry into the Promised Land was to be through trusting Him alone.

Joshua and Caleb saw not the strength of their enemies but the goodness of the land. They wanted nothing else than to return to the land that they spied out, the land that the Lord had given them as a gift.

In Joshua and Caleb's eyes, their enemies were their bread.[149] After tasting the goodness of the Promised Land when they spied it out, they became possessed by it!

In the midst of all this distrust and chaos, and right at the point when the Israelites were about to stone Caleb and Joshua, the glory of the Lord appeared and saved them from martyrdom.

> The promise of the kingdom of God is given to every believer; but how many are discouraged by the difficulties in the way! A slothful heart sees dangers, lions, and giants, everywhere; and therefore refuses to proceed in the heavenly path. Many of the spies contribute to this by the bad reports they bring of the heavenly country.
>
> Certain preachers allow "that the land is good, that it flows with milk and honey," and go so far as to show some of its fruits; but they discourage the people by stating the impossibility of overcoming their enemies. "Sin," say they, "cannot be destroyed in this life—it will always dwell in you—the Anakim cannot be conquered—we are but as grasshoppers against the Anakim," etc., etc.
>
> Here and there a Joshua and a Caleb, trusting alone in the power of God, armed with faith in the infinite efficacy of that blood which cleanses from all unrighteousness, boldly stand forth and say: "Their defense is departed from them, and the Lord

is with us; let us go up at once and possess the land, for we are well able to overcome."

We can do all things through Christ strengthening us: he will purify us unto himself, and give us that rest from sin here which his death has procured and his word has promised.

Reader, canst thou not take God at his word? He has never yet failed thee. Surely then thou hast no reason to doubt. Thou hast never yet tried him to the uttermost. Thou knowest not how far and how fully he can save.[150]

It is astounding to see such unbelief in the hearts of the children of Israel. It is equally astounding to see how fast and wholly it spread; it infected the Israelites like a plague running rampant throughout their camp.

These were God's own special people. It was they who were chosen to bear His name and carry His covenant.[151] They all saw staggering displays of the supernatural; yet here, their sin was that after all these miraculous demonstrations they simply did not trust.

To them, God's promise and their entry into it seemed too good to be true—just too easy.

Truly, not only was the way of entry designed to be with ease but also the land itself was filled with effortless prosperity. It truly was "a land flowing (issuing) with milk and honey!"[152]

The "Promised Land" that the Lord was to give to the Israelites, was a country filled with cities that they did not build.[153] It was full of vineyards they did not plant and houses full of good things that they did not buy.

The Lord gave them this opportunity to trust Him and enter at once into the land that He had promised them. This was a magnificent land flowing with provision and prosperity. Yet, they did not take the easy way of trust.

Their punishment was that they would spend forty years wandering in the desert, a year for every day that the spies were in the land, until all the ones who distrusted and cried out against the Lord in unbelief were dead. They would wander until all their corpses were scattered in the desert.[154]

The Lord said that they would "bear their own guilt."

I believe the rebellion of these Israelites was not one of disobedience, but of distrust. They knew the power and might of Jehovah, they saw His wonders, yet they shunned the ease of their entry. They did not enter in by faith.

> So we see that they were not able to enter [into His rest], because of their unwillingness to adhere to and trust in and rely on God [unbelief had shut them out].[155]

In these forty years that the Israelites wandered, we see the mercy of the Lord resting upon His people. In the desert years, the Lord provided absolutely everything supernaturally. The Lord provided water out of a rock, manna, quail, even clothes and sandals that never wore out,[156] all examples of His fathomless mercies to a rebellious people.

But although they were living in the mercies of the Lord, they were not living in His promise! This must have constantly been upon the minds and hearts of the children of Israel, as part of their self-inflicted punishment.

As we look at this in light of the work of Christ, we should not make the same mistake of unbelief that Israel did.

What was promised through thousands of years of patriarchs and prophets has been fulfilled in the giving of Christ. He alone has defeated the giants; He alone has carried us across the Jordan into the Promised Land of salvation.

These things were recorded for us, in order that we not shun the ease of entry that the Gospel offers.

> How many are retarded in their course, and fall short of the blessings of the Gospel, through magnifying the number and strength of their adversaries, their own weakness and the difficulties of the way with which we may connect their distrust of the power, faithfulness, and goodness of God! And how many are prevented from receiving the higher degrees of salvation by foolishly attributing insurmountable power, either to their inward corruptions or outward enemies! Only such men as Joshua and Caleb, who take God at his word, and who know that against his wisdom no cunning can stand, and against his might no strength can prevail, are likely to follow God fully, and receive the heights, lengths, breadths, and depths of the salvation of God.[157]

The writer of Hebrews tells us that the *Good News* has been preached unto us, just as it was to the Israelites that day.[158]

What was that *Good News* or *Gospel* that was preached to them? It was that they could enter into the Promised Land at once, and for all, by faith! They needed no swords nor military might, only childlike trust in their God.

The same Good News is available to us today. At once and for all, we may enter into the Land of the Promise, set free from the slavery of sin. We need only trust in Christ's giant-defeating sacrifice. Rivers of milk and honey are ours if we simply trust our God!

If this way seems too radical and too good, let it be accredited to the radical love and goodness of God, who wants nothing more than to see His children enter into what He has given them as a gift. The Gospel will always shock us with ease and surprise us with joy!

Hebrews also says that they did not enter into the rest that was promised because they did not mix their faith with Joshua and Caleb.[159] Let us mix our faith with those who do believe and go in at once. We should not distrust the Lord by making the way impassable and impossible. This way has been opened for us through the rent veil of our Messiah's body!

Yes, the way is straight and the road is narrow. It is the way of faith; childlike trust in Christ and His cross.

You may say, "Aren't you making Christianity just too easy?"

I would answer that I have devoted my life to preaching the effortlessness of the Gospel and the work of the cross, and I am convinced that my lips have not yet matched the reality of its ease.

+ Are We DREAMING?

Some might say: "Wake up; you're dreaming! The kind of Christianity you are describing sounds great, but it does not exist."

It is likely that you also are saying this right about now. That's OK; it's a normal reaction. Don't worry; there's nothing wrong with you.

Let us look at Psalm 126. It is by far one of my most favorite psalms. Again, we see in this psalm that God's salvation seems almost too good to be true.

> *It seemed like a dream, too good to be true, when God returned Zion's exiles. We laughed, we sang, we couldn't believe our good fortune. We were the talk of the nations—"God was wonderful to them!" God was wonderful to us; we are one happy people.*[160]

Here the people of God are staggered by their deliverance. They felt it must have been a dream.

> *"When the Lord turned again the captivity of Zion, we were like them that dream."* Being in trouble, the gracious pilgrims remember for their comfort times of national woe which were succeeded by remarkable deliverances. Then sorrow was gone like a dream, and the joy which followed was so great that it seemed too good to be true, and they feared that it must be the vision of an idle brain. So sudden and so overwhelming was their joy that they felt like men out of themselves, ecstatic, or in a trance. The captivity had been great, and great was the deliverance; for the great God himself had wrought it: it seemed too good to be actually true: each man said to himself, "Is this a dream? O if it be a dream, Let me sleep on, and do not wake me yet."[161]

But it was not a dream; it was reality!

This psalm is a song of rapture. The children of Israel were swiftly and sovereignly delivered from their slavery.

So it is with us!

The salvation that the Lord provides through His Son, Jesus the Christ, is a swift and sovereign one. Salvation from sin in this life seems like a dream, too good to be true. But this, my friends, is what salvation truly is—salvation from the slavery of sin.

Why should we expect anything less from such a loving God as we have? Be stunned by the deliverance, but let it turn into song and laughter.

> *Then was our mouth filled with laughter, and our tongue with singing….* So full were they of joy that they could not contain themselves. They must express their joy and yet they could not find expression for it. Irrepressible mirth could do no other than laugh, for speech was far too dull a thing for it. The mercy was so unexpected, so amazing, so singular that they could not do less than laugh; and they laughed much, so that their mouths were full of it, and that because their hearts were full, too. When at last the tongue could move articulately, it could not be content simply to talk, but it must needs sing; and sing heartily too, for it was full of singing. Doubtless the former pain added to the zest of the pleasure; the captivity threw a brighter color into the emancipation. The people remembered this joy flood for years after, and here is the record of it turned into a song.[162]

Respond to this magnificent salvation, not with reservation but with laughter and singing. If you do this, God will laugh and sing along with you! He Himself will teach you the melodies of praise that you were created to sing.

> *God turns life around. Turned-around Jacob skips rope, turned-around Israel sings laughter.*[163]

YOUR NOTES=

_____

_____

_____

_____

_____

_____

_____

_____

_____

_____

_____

_____

_____

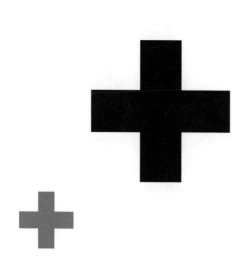

08

+ THE LANGUAGE, MADNESS, AND MYSTICISM OF APOSTLE PAUL

What does this "New Creation Reality" sound like from a man's lips?

Oh, it is overwhelmingly wonderful when this truth sets a heart free and gives him a new language to speak; when the language of the New Creation plants itself deeply into his heart.

As we read the letters of the apostle Paul and listen to the language he speaks, we are quickly drawn to a higher realm. His language differs exponentially from any other biblical writer. Not that the others are disqualified by any means, but the apostle Paul seems to be speaking from a higher viewpoint. When we look through the Word with "Pauline eyes" everything black and white turns to technicolor. The crude outlines and scribbles turn into magnificent masterpieces—portraits of Christ crucified. Everything turns from black and white to portraits of Christ crucified.

+ The **MADNESS** of Paul

The apostle Paul was a raving madman, consumed in boasting about what Christ had accomplished on the cross.

He was forbidden to speak or to pride himself in any other thing save from that blissful cross.[164] In his letters, he ecstatically declares and frolics in the revelation of Christ, almost in a blabbering manner, sometimes overcome by the sheer pleasure of the Gospel!

Festus told him "his much learning had made him mad."[165] Oh, but if Festus only knew how mad Paul really was!

Paul says in Second Corinthians 5:13,*"If I am standing outside myself in ecstasy, it is because of God."*[166]

And, *"If I'm off my rocker, it's for God."*[167]

But there was a glorious reason for Paul's madness. Paul was mad about the Gospel!

> *Paul became completely possessed by the message.*[168]

He was crazy about the cross!

In the next verse, Second Corinthians 5:14, we read why Paul was beside himself. Paul says that the love of Christ gave him *"an impelling motive, namely that one has died on behalf of all, therefore all have died."*[169]

The unstoppable love force of God, which he discovered in the Gospel, drove Paul's madness.

The love of Christ had *"overmastered him,"*[170] as the Weymouth translation puts it.

The *"love of Christ left him no choice"*[171] but to believe that he had shared in Christ's death.

Paul's eyes had become opened to the reality that he had participated in the crucifixion of Christ, and this revelation had possessed him. This was the fount of the ecstasies of Paul. This was the source of his madness and his shocking language.

+ The MYSTICISM of Paul

Paul had been given a divine drive to spread to the entire world the mystical realities of the Gospel. He was a dispenser of a new dimension and a new world. This dimension was Christ and His New Covenant.

Paul was a *"dispenser of the mysteries of God."*[172] The apostle Paul was the first mystic theologian.

> Mysterion appears twenty-one times in Paul's letters out of a total of twenty-seven NT occurrences....Paul normally employs the term with reference to its disclosure or its being revealed.[173]

So what is this mystic secret that has now been revealed?

> *...know more definitely and accurately and thoroughly that mystic secret of God, [which is] Christ (the Anointed One).*[174]

The mystery is Christ and the reality of our union with Him.

It seems that this mystery was hidden throughout the ages from angels and from men but has now, through the epistles of Paul, been revealed to those who believe.

The basis of Paul's mysticism is the reality of the believer dying, being buried, and rising with Christ. His letters and language are filled with this mystical union.

> Paul mystically identifies the believers with Christ and figuratively describes the process of salvation in the Christian man in terms of the saving deeds which procured his salvation—in and with the saving deeds—Christ's death and resurrection—the salvation of all believers is conceived of as accomplished, so that the believing world is described as dying (to sin) when Christ died, and as rising with him to newness of life. This method of thought is the supreme example of Paul's mysticism.[175]

It is clear that even Paul's ecstatic experiences were based on and produced by a revelation of the truth, as he says:

> *Fourteen years ago I was the subject of an incomprehensible ecstasy, in which truths too great for human language were imparted to me. I will base my boast on such experiences in which*

I was but the dependent, passive instrument of the Lord.[176]

I read this and I believed that I also could be the subject of the same incomprehensible ecstasy, *"in which truths too great for human language were imparted to me."*

It would do you well to believe the same!

If you truly believe that you have died with Christ, it follows that you will undoubtedly and irresistibly fall into the ecstasy of your new life.

This is the joy of mystical union!

It is the ecstasy of salvation!

Though Paul speaks of this truth that was imparted to him as "beyond language" or "forbidden" to speak, it is evident that this truth oozes into what he did write. Though it was forbidden to speak, the revelation was obviously leaking out of his whole being.

One question that quickly rises to the forefront of our minds and hearts when we read such things in the Scripture is this: *Do we base our boast upon ecstatic experiences?*

This is what the apostle says: "I will base my boast on such experiences in which I was but the dependent, passive instrument of the Lord."

Paul was the dependent, passive recipient of an ecstatic experience in which came a divine revelation. I believe that the ecstasy was both the vehicle that the Lord used to impart the revelation, and it was the product of the revelation.

Divine joy and divine revelation should never be divorced. The news should never be separated from its goodness, for it is the Good News!

If the ecstatic experience were stripped from the Gospel message, it would be just another distant promise. But the fact is that the two cannot be separated, for in the fabric of the Gospel we find woven and intertwined such doses of joy that it is impossible to describe in human language.

When the glad-message comes to you, you become the target of its gladness.

The Gospel pulls you out of your human senses and into heavenly ones—into the ecstasy of salvation.

Paul was downloaded with this heavenly revelation, which he was unable to fit into his very large and sophisticated vocabulary. It was beyond his ability to put it in words. It is because the Gospel speaks its own language, and it's not a human language.

The Gospel is not a human invention or idea—it's supernatural. It's a God invention. *"It's not a human message."*[177] Paul did not receive it from any man; it was divine revelation.[178]

Because the nature and origin of the Gospel is not human and from another realm, human methods can never attain it. It has to be gifted from that other realm.

We can only be the dependent, passive recipients of the Gospel. It can only be drunk down and received as a gift.

Yes, the apostle Paul was a mystic and an ecstatic. Yet his mysticism and raving ecstasies had their source in his revelation.

+ The LANGUAGE of Paul

Paul's language was one of a heart enraptured in full mystical union with Christ.

In the language of Paul, believers are described as having already shared in Christ's death, burial, and resurrection and are now enjoying union in His glorious reign. One of Paul's favorite phrases to describe this union is the phrase "in Christ."

In Paul's heart, he was inseparable from the Lord. He was one Spirit with Him.[179]

Paul's language is the language for the New Creation. You won't hear from Paul's lips some of the phrases that are commonly heard from many Christians.

In the New Creation language, you won't find longing and wanting. You will find endless praises declaring that the waiting and wanting is over. It's a language and song of blissful fulfillment and ecstatic satisfaction.

It is the New Song mentioned in the Psalms[180] and in Revelation.[181] It is the song of men made into the home of God, the song of mortals transformed and swallowed by Life.

+ LEARNING a New Language

The language of the New Creation is the inner realities of the heart spoken out loud for all to hear and be made jealous. It declares, "I have already been crucified with Christ." It sings, "I am altogether new." It boasts in the revelation of what Christ has accomplished.

Isn't it heart-rending that so many believers don't know how to speak this language? They are stuck in the undone, instead of floating upon the finished.

Some of the phrases of the old language are:

"I must nail myself to the cross every day."

"I'm just a sinner saved by grace."

"Lord, You saved me but now come and cleanse me," or "Every day I've got to die to my flesh."

Obviously the list goes on, and for the sheer fact that I hate hearing them, I will say no more of these faithless jabberings. This is a dead language!

It should not exist for the believer. Our language should always be a boast and praise that Christ has provided a perfect cure to our once-separated condition. We should revel and frolic like Paul in our newfound union with Christ. We should be like blabbering madmen filled with God's kind of righteousness. We should be believers who can't shut up about the New Creation realities!

Those who speak this new language have been captivated by the revelation that they were once for all nailed to His cross, and this not at their hand or by their will, but by the sovereign will of the happy God.

Yes, we were sinners, but now we are saints!

We weren't saved and forgiven to remain in the sinful state that we were in—we were translated out of the kingdom of darkness into the Kingdom of Christ's light and love.[182]

If we don't see this, we miss salvation's purpose and its bliss.

If we have no clue what we were saved from, then in turn we cannot know what we're saved into.

Listen to Paul's language concerning "the flesh" and let it give you new terminology:

> In Him also you were circumcised with a circumcision not made with hands, but in a [spiritual] circumcision [performed by] Christ by stripping off the body of the flesh (the whole corrupt, carnal nature with its passions and lusts).[183]

The apostle Paul always points to the *"you were"* circumcised and the old *"has been"* cut away when speaking about the flesh and the old sinful existence.

Our language as Christians should not be a mixture of old and new, it should be like Paul's—a pure and strong drink of the truth.

> ...From now on, think of it this way: Sin speaks a dead language that means nothing to you; God speaks your mother tongue, and you hang on every word....[184]

I believe that many still speak that old, dead language simply out of ignorance. I say that in the sense that they have simply never heard the new language offered by the finished work of Christ.

They just have never had a chance to believe it! This is a tragedy on the part of the ministers of the Gospel.

So, listen with the ears of your heart. Listen intently to the sweet truth being proclaimed through the Gospel. Let the Lord minister to you the scroll that is sweet like honey.[185] Let that sweetness enlighten your eyes like it did Jonathan's.[186]

Feast, like Jeremiah, on Heaven's Word, and let it become your delight.

> *Your words were found, and I ate them, and Your words became to me a joy and the delight of my heart....*[187]

Let the realities stir in the deepest parts of your heart. Let the new become real to you.

Simply submit and surrender to God's way of salvation.

The new language is the language of faith, which is trust.[188] It's the language of love, not longing.

Yes, you were once lovesick, but Love Himself came and cured that disease. What you hungered for, Christ became and was given to you for your satisfaction.

I ask, if we are not completely satisfied with Christ's offering on the cross, with what will we be?

Know this, God Himself is completely and supremely satisfied with Christ's sacrifice. Let that wonderful sacrifice drive you mad like it did Paul. Let the song of satisfaction come to your lips.

Come joyously to the same conclusion that Paul did:

> That One died on behalf of all, therefore all have died with Him.[189]

When this reality hits you, it will instantly change your native tongue. You will blissfully forget how to speak the old, and you will be overcome with the new. Then and only then will the true praises roll effortlessly off your tongue.

Frequencies of heavenly bliss are yours, and as a New Creation you must respond to the revelation of the Gospel by singing and boasting in them.

YOUR NOTES=

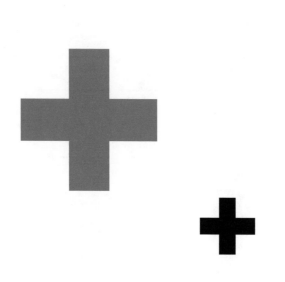

09

+ **EFFORTLESS** CHRISTIANITY

So where do our efforts belong in all of this?

What is our place as Christians?

Our place in Christianity is simply to be His—to be in Christ.

Just surrender to what He has done.

Surrender to mystical union!

There are some amazing things that take place when you recognize your union with Christ. You begin to notice that love comes when you least expect it, and flows to the most unlikely of suspects.

Instead of throwing insults, you find yourself throwing hugs.

A holy life becomes a simple outflow of love.

Things, for which we once worked so hard, now come to us so effortlessly.

We must *realize* that we are one with Christ, and that we take part in *His attributes* only because we have partaken *of Him*.

As true Christians, we must become conscious of our total and absolute dependence upon Christ. Our hearts are in His hands completely; it is He who holds us to Himself.

Our efforts are not necessary to produce the desired Christian life. The Wuest translation of Second Corinthians 5:14 says: *"For the love which Christ has for me holds me to one end, prohibiting me from considering any other."*[190]

The King James Version of this verse says: *"the love of Christ constraineth us."*[191]

"Constraineth" is *sunecho* in Greek. It means "to hold together lest it fall to pieces, to press on every side, of a strait that forces a ship into a narrow channel, of a cattle squeeze forcing the beast into a position where the farmer can administer medication, of a besieged city, to possess."[192]

Wow, all that for one word! It is Christ's love that holds us together, lest we fall to pieces. His love forces us into the narrow way. It is His love that prohibits us from wanting any other.

Christianity becomes effortless when we realize that Christ possesses us! Christ's love has besieged our hearts so much in that, no other goods but His pass through our gates.

We have been crucified with Christ.[193] The work has been done, and the cure imparted to us!

We are not held to salvation by our efforts or sustained by our striving; we are held by Christ's heart-melting love and fed from His perfect sacrifice.

God not only saved us single-handedly but also sustains us single-handedly.

He really *does* have the *whole world in His hands!*

+ Married to GRACE

There are many distortions and misunderstandings floating around in the Christian world concerning the work of Christ and the work of the believer.

Let me put this into a picture, the same picture and language that the apostle Paul used:

Those who demand to please the Lord through effort and Law, heartbreakingly miss out on the benefits of being married to grace. Being Christians, they should enjoy being wedded to grace, but instead they are committing adultery with the Law.

Or maybe the problem lies in that some don't realize that they are now released from the Law, and are free to marry grace?

> *Wherefore, my brethren, ye also are become dead to the law by the body of Christ; that ye should be married to another, even to Him who is raised from the dead, that we should bring forth fruit unto God.[194]*

In fact, not only did we die to the Law through the crucified body of Christ, but also the Law itself died!

This is how the Wuest translation puts it:

> *So, my brethren, to you also the Law died through the incarnation of Christ, that you might be wedded to Another, namely to Him who rose from the dead in order that we might yield fruit to God.*[195]

Granted, most Christians are clueless about Judaic Law and obviously don't keep its requirements. But many still follow in that same spirit of the struggle of the Law, striving for acceptance with God through self-efforts.

The Jewish Law was meant to convince humanity that keeping it was utterly impossible without the indwelling presence of God.

In fact, it was given to increase the consciousness of indwelling sin:"The introduction of the law caused sin to increase."[196]

Galatians 3:24-25 describes the Law as our tutor until faith came, or until Christ came, as it seems in this Scripture that faith and Christ are interchangeable.

The Law is our tutor because it leads us to the realization that we need a Savior. The Law makes us realize that we cannot live the life that God requires without Christ!

And here is where grace makes its magnificent entry!

> But where sin abounded, the gift of grace has overflowed beyond the outbreak of sin.[197]

> *Sin is shown to be wide and deep, thank God His grace is wider and deeper still.*[198]

And the Good News is that Christ alone, dwelling in our hearts, enables us to live out that holy and happy life that God desires.

This is the glorious difference between Christianity and religion. This is the difference between Christ and the Law.

We are now married to another!

Where religion and the Law cannot go, Christ has gone. Where your self-efforts end, Christ's work truly begins.

Though many of these religious and moral laws have intentions that are truly good and noble, they cannot make a people righteous. None but Christ can impart to humankind the gift of living out what God requires.

This change in our nature happens to us, not by us. Christ does not need our permission to make this change in our hearts. He just wants us to respond with belief at what He has done for us.

Christ came to destroy sin through giving His life! This was His purpose; it was why He was manifested in flesh. Sin began in skin, blood, and bone. So Christ was manifested in a body, with skin, blood, and with bones. He was made the scapegoat that carried our sinfulness to the wilderness.

> He used His servant body to carry our sins to the cross so we could be rid of sin, free to live the right way. His wounds became your healing.[199]

Where sin began, in the Adamic nature, in the same, The Christ has abolished it!

> For what was impossible to the Law—powerless as it was because it acted through frail humanity—God effected. Sending His own Son in a body like that of sinful human nature and as a sacrifice for sin, He pronounced sentence upon sin in human nature.[200]

Christ united Himself with *our humanity and destroyed sin.* This is a cause of endless rejoicing!

Glorious Good News has come to our doors with a wonderful surprise—union with God has miraculously been achieved!

Through our union with Christ, *sin's cruel rule over our hearts has finally ended. Unification with Christ means nothing less than the end of the domination of sin.* Love is now our divine master. The whip of guilt and shame no longer drive us.

God has done it! He really has done it!

He made Himself one with us. The ladder to Heaven that none could climb has fallen down. Christ has descended to us to lift us into the heavenlies with Him.

He was the bright-red and delicious apple high in the tree. We couldn't climb—so He fell to us. And effortlessly we eat of what He has done. This is the destination that all arrive at, after one sip of the Pure Gospel.

We realize that Heaven is not earned; it is given. The only efforts necessary for this union with God were Christ's. Just simply respond with childlike wonder and amazement at the work of Christ. Just shout, *"Yes, I believe it!"*

Let faith burst from the seams of your heart!

+ The Day of ATONEMENT

In Leviticus chapter 23, we see how the Lord is jealous about the Day of Atonement.

This is the one day a year when the priest would sprinkle blood upon the mercy seat and Israel's sins would be covered.

On this day, the Lord commanded no one to work at all.[201] In fact, if He found them working on the Day of Atonement they would be destroyed.[202]

When I read this Scripture, I realized that not only are our efforts unnecessary, they are not allowed! This Scripture shows how serious the Lord is about a hands-free salvation. He alone is salvation's benefactor. As His creatures, we must submit to this salvation and not rebel against His way of righteousness.

Though shocked by the ease of it, we should not shun it! We must yield to the ease and effortlessness of the Gospel. We, like the Israelites on the Day of Atonement, must surrender to the divine grace of Jehovah.

The Day of Atonement for the Jews now is a sober day of mourning and depression, I believe because of the uncertainty of their forgiveness (though historically the Day of Atonement was filled with the joys of Jehovah's mercies).

To me, this day paints such a wonderful picture of Christ and His work on the cross.

> The ecstatic joy, which is absent from the contemporary experience of Yom Kippur (or day of atonement), is taken for granted in the Talmud (book of rabbinic discussion on the Law and customs of the Jews).
>
> The experience of Yom Kippur was palatably different in Temple times. We are told that there was a red string in the Temple that turned white, serving as a veritable spiritual barometer

of God's forgiveness of man. When the people were shown this tangible sign of forgiveness, celebration erupted.

Rabbi Yishmael said: "But they had another sign too; a thread of crimson wool was tied to the door of the Temple, and when the goat reached the wilderness, the thread turned white. As it is written: 'Though your sins be as scarlet they shall be as white as snow.'" (Yoma 68b)

This type of joy was spontaneous, even though it was a yearly occurrence on Yom Kippur. Singing, dancing and celebration broke out all over. The women of Jerusalem would dance in the vineyards.[203]

On the head of the scape-goat a piece of scarlet cloth was tied, and the tradition of the Jews states that if God accepted the sacrifice the scarlet cloth turned white while the goat was led to the desert; but if God had not accepted this expiation, the redness continued, and the rest of the year was spent in mourning.[204]

And the ancient Hebrews write, that forty years before the destruction of the temple, which was about the time of Christ's death, this red string turned no more white.[205]

Tradition holds that Jesus was resurrected in white garments, as He had supernaturally passed through the grave clothes that He had left in the tomb.

This tells me that when Jesus' bloody red body was resurrected in white garments of glory, it was our proof forever that our atonement at the cross was complete!

Let the joy of atonement once again explode in the people of God.

Let our hearts now erupt with unquenchable joy! Let the celebration be heard for hundreds of miles! With mouths full of laughter, let's shout the praises until every ear on Earth is ringing with the bliss of the Gospel.

Our atonement is complete!

+ The SIN-BEARER

It is apparent, through many portions of Scripture, that God does not require our self-works and performance to produce acceptance with Him.

What He does desire is a childlike response to His work upon the cross. The Phillips Translation says in Acts 17:11 that, *"… the whole matter is now on a different plane—believing instead of achieving."*[206]

We see in some Scripture stories that the message of the Gospel and of Christ is almost pre-told. It is like the Lord was giving sneak peeks into the story of redemption. The Exegeses Translation calls it *"pre-evangelism."*[207]

One of these previews is in the story of Cain and Abel. Cain, we see in Genesis chapter 4, offered a sacrifice from the produce of his hands, tilling and working the cursed ground. But Abel offered a firstling from his flock, which was a type of Christ.

> *The Lord had respect unto Abel and to his offering.*[208]

The word *respect* is *shaw-aw*. It means "to gaze or to look upon."[209] The Lord looked upon Abel's offering but could not look or gaze at Cain's offering.

The writer of Hebrews says that by faith Abel offered a better sacrifice.[210] Why was it a better sacrifice? It was because Abel offered in faith, not from the self-works of his hands.

When we bring a sacrifice from the works of our hands seeking right standing, the Lord cannot even look at it. All He will accept is Christ's offering.

The passage in Genesis 4 goes on to say that the Lord spoke to Cain and said, *"If you do well, will you not be accepted?"*[211]

I believe this means, *"Don't you realize that if you bring to Me the correct sacrifice, the one of faith, that you will be accepted?"*

The Lord speaks on in the passage, and here is where we see the awesome mercy of the Lord on grand display.

The King James Version says, *"If thou doest not well, sin lieth at the door."* In fact, this is not the true meaning of the Hebrew words. This is not a warning that sin is ready to pounce upon Cain; it is an extension to Cain of the grace of God.

The word for "sin" here is *chattaah*,[212] which does not mean sin in this instance but "sin-offering."[213]

And "lieth" is *rabats* and is defined as "to crouch on all four legs like a recumbent animal."[214]

The Lord here is actually saying to Cain, "If you did not do well, in that you did not offer the sacrifice I required, a sin-offering (Christ the lamb) is lying on all fours waiting at the entrance of your door, ready to be sacrificed."

See the endless mercy of the Lord! He showed Cain a sacrifice that would be accepted, even after Cain had failed.

A much better translation comes from both the Young's Literal and the Rotherham translations:

Young's Literal Translation: *"...and if thou dost not well, at the opening a sin-offering is crouching."*[215]

Rotherham's: *"But, if thou do not right, at the entrance, a sin-bearer is lying...."*[216]

Adam Clarke's Commentary says:

> ...a sin-offering lieth at the door; an animal proper to be offered as an atonement for sin is now crouching at the door of thy fold...God now graciously informs him that, though he had miscarried, his case was not yet desperate.

If we offer to the Lord that which He requires, we will be accepted, and all that He requires is His Son, Jesus the Christ.

Offer to God what has been ordained to be offered before the foundation of time. Offer to Him not of the fruits and produce of your efforts, but offer to Him your childlike faith in what He has accomplished on the cross. Offer to Him the Lamb who was slain, that is lying in wait at your door.

> *Behold, I stand at the door and knock: if any man hear My voice, and open the door, I will come in to him, and will sup with him, and he with Me.*[217]

For the Sin-Bearer lies crouched at our doors, ready to justify.

+ This Changes **EVERYTHING!**

Let me put forth a simple truth—God does not need our help when it comes to our salvation!

This is a simple yet revolutionary truth. This changes everything!

The ancient question of man is: *"What should we do?"*[218]

The answer from Heaven has always been: *"This is the only work God wants from you: Believe in the one He has sent."*[219]

Believing upon the joyful message of what Christ has done is all that God really wants of us.

The Great Gospel of imparted righteousness is in continual orbit around the slain Lamb, like the living creatures surrounding the throne continually singing, "Holy, Holy, Holy." All of Heaven is enraptured in the ecstasy of His holiness and astonished that this holiness has been graced to us!

This holiness and righteousness are not attained by self-submission and self-obedience. No, this righteousness can only be drunk down as a gift.

No other kind of righteousness can stand before His presence. What we have been given is a righteousness that is unearned and unachieved. It is a glorious gift! This gift is what the Gospel imparts to those who believe.

I believe that a holy life, the enjoyment of it, and its outflow to others, *is* the evidence of Christianity. But many other things are mistaken to be sole evidence of Kingdom life.

Some are twisted ideas that measure nearness to the Lord by gifts of miracles, heavenly encounters, or abilities. Such notions leave room only for self-achievement, self-attainment, and eventually self-disappointment. When one gives the heart over to such a system of believing, he or she forgets the very heart of the true Gospel, which is simple and childlike faith.

Instead of trusting in the ability of God, we find ourselves in a place where our efforts are needed to produce the desired result, whether it is miracles, holiness, or any other good thing.

All of us are guilty of this subtle mesmerizing of the soul, but as subtle as it may be, it leads to a polluted and stagnant pool. Surrendering to such ideas build up for us a kingdom made of salt and castles made of sand, which inevitably falls with the changing of the wind.

In saying that, let me emphasize that of course miracles do come. But they come at the call of faith. The miraculous is the portion of every believer.[220] Jesus said that signs and wonders would follow those who believe upon the Gospel. The miraculous follows the Gospel!

If you aren't seeing evidence of the miraculous in your life, you shouldn't be asking the question: *"What else do I need to do?"* But rather, you should be asking: *"What Gospel am I preaching?"*

With its stunning offer of unending blessings, the Gospel is the greatest miracle of all time! It not only gives to us healing, but it gives us wholeness, filling our spirits, souls, and bodies.

The Gospel declares to us that Christ abides with us and in us always, by faith. He once and for all opened the heavens for all to drink their fill. All of the storehouses of the miraculous have been blasted open and given to us in the giving of Christ.

These blessings of the Gospel are not just for the few who can press in for them. No, they are for all who believe!

Don't ever take your eyes off the grand miracle of a life possessed by God!

When the sweet truth of the Gospel arrests our hearts, we set sail on an endless ocean of bliss. The measuring rod of comparison is tossed overboard. The storms of unfulfillment and disappointment disintegrate into nothing.

No longer let down by the lack of seeing the miraculous, we are absorbed in a gaze at *The Miracle—Christ*. Heaven becomes the wind in our sails, and signs and wonders ripple endlessly behind us. We sing the melody of faith endlessly and joyously, like a drunken sailor singing after having too much rum.

Let this same song be yours! Let it drip from your lips like sticky honey dripping from the comb. Let all taste its sweetness and become addicted to its effect upon their hearts.

YOUR NOTES=

10

+ THE HAPPY CHRISTIAN

A happy Christian?

What?

Rarely are the words *happy* and *Christian* put together.

Happiness is the full intent of the Lord, and it is the effect that the Gospel has upon the heart of humankind.

God loves joy!

The reason He loves joy is because He is infinitely joyful.

The word for "blessed" is *makarios* in Greek. It is in fact defined as "happy."[221] It is used as one of the names of God in First Timothy 1:11 (*Makarios Theos*—The Happy God!).

Yes, our God is the happy God! And His message is a message of supreme gladness. He is the Source of all true bliss and happiness; to be near to Him is to be near to an atomic bomb of joy!

Go ahead...press the red button. You know you want to!

If you lack this joy that I have been describing, maybe it's simply because it has never been offered to you. What I mean is that the Gospel may have never been presented to you in its irresistible goodness. You may have never heard such wonderful things as are written in this book.

One current, joy-robbing idea of Christianity is that it is little more than a new start on an old life—just a second chance.

If this is true, that Christianity is simply a new beginning at the same old kind of life, what makes me think that I'm not going to make a mess of it again?

The "old life," our pre-Christ existence, was filled with sinfulness and the inability to choose God even if we desired to. Even if we had been given a new start, it would still be the "old life"!

But what Christ gives us is a "new life" in quality, a new kind of life. It is not the same kind of life just patched up a bit, with a few moral guidelines to keep us on the straight and narrow. We have entered into a new world full of love and life. We've fallen heart-first into endless rivers of holy enjoyment.

Jesus said you couldn't put a new piece of cloth on an old garment. And you cannot pour new, vibrant, and living wine into an old wineskin.[222] The two cannot go together.

No wonder so many Christians have a joy deficiency. The "old life" and joy cannot coexist.

And the truth is that you are not the same old you; you are a New Creation living in a new world.

Absolutely everything is new!

I don't know about you, but this makes me happy! In fact, I feel like doing cartwheels right now!

> *I'm singing joyful praise to God. I'm turning cartwheels of joy to my Savior God.*[223]

The "old life" has been destroyed. You can dig as much as you want, but you will find no remnants of this "old life" buried in the Gospel! This makes joy and happiness come effortlessly for the believer.

Happy Christianity is God's idea! It requires as much effort as it takes a man dying of thirst in the desert to drink from an oasis.

And Christ is that oasis. He is the Rock that was struck and is forever exploding with the pure, truly satiating drink. This torrent needs help from none. It gushes and spills itself out freely.

The miracle of joy happens when we realize the gift of Christ. The effect, when you are in union with Him, is that you become a partaker also of all that He is. You become one with His divine nature.

The nature of the happy God—is happiness. So it is also for the one indwelt by Him.

When we know and realize that Christ is our joy, we cannot help but be joyful. His nature is imparted and implanted into the heart that has been mastered by Him.

Individuals who can clearly see their union with Christ are persons bursting at the seams with joy! Ransomed from a life of sin and sadness, those individuals sing never-ending songs of laughter to the Savior.

They worship their happy God—with happiness!

> *The people God has ransomed will come back on this road. They'll sing as they make their way home to Zion, unfading halos of joy encircling their heads, welcomed home with gifts of joy and gladness as all sorrows and sighs scurry into the night.*[224]

+ FEASTING On Christ

Seeing the Gospel in such glorious light, and in view of the realities that are pouring out of the epistles of Paul, I am left with this conclusion—Christianity is not a fast; it is a festival!

It is a feast!

I understand this may sound like a foreign idea to many, but it is the simple truth!

My intention is not necessarily to disqualify fasting. It is more to amplify the need to *feast* upon Christ's sacrifice, while also redefining what true fasting is.

I know that this is most likely opposite to what most of us have been taught, but allow me to clarify, before you are shocked beyond the point of no return.

Marriage, I believe, is a wonderful example of our union with the Lord—I love my wife with all my heart; she is all mine and

I am completely hers. When I want to feel that nearness, I simply spend time with her.

It is the same with the Lord. If you want to feel closer to Him, simply spend time feasting on what He did for you on the cross. Spend time feasting upon His finished works, and you will without a doubt become aware of His nearness to you and your union with Him.

Sometimes seeing how much you already have overshadows what you think you need.

The Lord spoke to an anonymous mystic and said, "If I am in you, and you are in me, and I am closer than the air you breathe, then why are you still looking for me?"[225]

Are you also still looking for Him? Just simply awaken to mystical union through the work of the cross!

If for some reason you are not feeling the closeness of this union, maybe you are not approaching Him on His terms. Christianity can't be on our own terms, offering up sacrifices that seem right to us, in hopes of becoming nearer to Jesus. It is simply not His way.

The way is straight and the road is narrow—it is only by His cross!

If you want more of Jesus, then just have Him! He gave Himself to us unreservedly.

What are we waiting for?

Maybe it's that we just don't realize what real Christianity is?

The current, common idea of Christianity is one of lifelong, rigorous self-mortification and longing. *Feasting* and *joy* are words that are simply not in most Christians' vocabularies.

For most Christians, the only hope for pleasure and joy is that one day we will pass through those pearly white gates, receive our halos, and float around on white clouds while staring at rainbows for eternity.

This, my friend, is not the Heaven Christ offers!

It seems even our idea of Heaven has been infected by religion. Heaven's enamoring is not with bizarre beings and crystal seas, though these are truly amazing and wonder-filled.

We, who have been bought in blood, will be captivated with the sight of the Lamb. All of Heaven worships inward toward the Lamb, who is in the very midst of the throne. Such pleasure radiates from this Lamb, that all of Heaven's citizens fall to their faces, overcome with the sheer bliss of seeing Him.

All stare awestruck, in glory, at the slain Lamb, seeing that He still bears the marks of the crucifixion.

> And I saw in the midst of the throne and of the four living beings and in the midst of the elders, a Lamb standing, [in appearance] like a lamb that has been slain [bearing the wounds of the cross in His glorified body]....[226]

The slain Lamb is the bliss of Heaven! This is the true pleasure that Heaven holds. Christ, God's Lamb, is what makes Heaven, Heaven.

And the wonderful promise of the Gospel is that we need not wait for this pleasure to be realized. God, with all of His joys, has made our hearts His home. He is not "God far away" or "God far off." He is Immanuel, "God *with* us!"

We have God now, and He has us. We are not searching for something we do not yet have, but we are exploring what has already been given to us as a gift.

Heaven *and Earth* are filled with His glory.[227] "Christ in us" is our hope of realizing that glory and Heaven's bliss now!

> *...the riches of the glory of this mystery, which is Christ within and among you, the Hope of [realizing the] glory.*[228]

We are the mystical Body of Christ, which is celebrating the advent of the revealing of the mystery—"Christ in us."

Yes, there was a time when the people of God fasted, when they longed for Christ.

But He has come! So let us feast upon Him!

Fasting seems almost always synonymous with sadness and mourning. It implies want and longing. This can in no way be the true expression of Christianity.

Fasting comes with tears, but the Gospel comes with laughter!

Listen to what Jesus said:

> *"...John the Baptist's disciples are constantly going without food, and praying...and so do the disciples of the Pharisees. Why are yours wining and dining?" Jesus asked, "Do happy men fast? Do wedding guests go hungry while celebrating with the groom?"*[229]

Do happy men fast?

He went on to say that there would be a time, or as the Living

Bible puts it, *"the time will come when the Bridegroom will be killed,"[230]* when the disciples would not feel like eating. That day was when He was crucified and was taken away from them!

But I have some wonderful news, friends—He is no longer taken from us; He is in us! Our fellowship with Him is unbroken.

> *Even so consider yourselves also dead to sin and your relation to it broken, but alive to God [living in unbroken fellowship with Him] in Christ Jesus.* [231]

Did you know that there is only one commanded fast in the entire Bible?[232] It was on the Day of Atonement, which is one of our greatest Old Testament pictures of Christ and His work on the cross.

This is also what Jesus is referring to in the previous Scripture that I mentioned in Luke—the true Day of Atonement, the day Christ was crucified.[233]

There is only one commanded *fast,* yet there are over seven major commanded *feasts* in the Bible, plus heaps of additional Jewish celebrations.

It seems very clear that the Lord desires us to serve Him with joy and celebration. We are even commanded in Deuteronomy to *"serve the Lord your God with a joyful and happy heart."[234]*

So what is true fasting?

Let us look at a Scripture that shines light on what *true* fasting is. In Isaiah, the Lord declares to us the fast that He desires:

> *Is such a fast as yours what I have chosen, a day for a man to humble himself with sorrow in his*

soul? [Is true fasting merely mechanical?] Is it only to bow down his head like a bulrush and to spread sackcloth and ashes under him [to indicate a condition of heart that he does not have]? Will you call this a fast and an acceptable day to the Lord? [Rather] is not this the fast that I have chosen: to loose the bonds of wickedness, to undo the bands of the yoke, to let the oppressed go free, and that you break every [enslaving] yoke? Is it not to divide your bread with the hungry and bring the homeless poor into your house—when you see the naked, that you cover him...?[235]

The fast that the Lord desires seems more like a big *feast!* It sounds like a party filled with food, mercy, and an invitation to the poor!

I have a wonderful idea...

Instead of declaring a 40-day fast, let's declare a 40-day feast and invite all of the poor!

In fact, that is what the preaching of the Gospel truly is—it is an invitation to a glorious festival. And whether you realize it or not, *we* were those poor who were invited to His table.[236] *We* were the lepers and rejected who were invited to His feast.

You should read the story of Mephibosheth in Second Samuel.[237] When I read his story, my heart melted at Jesus' mercy! We were like Mephibosheth—crippled and without family, yet mercifully changed from enemy into friend, from slave to son.

King David graciously brought Mephibosheth to his table, to a lifelong feast as one of his sons. The Lord has done for us the same that David did for Mephibosheth.

This is what Christianity holds for all who believe—an eternal seat at the table of the King, eating like an heir! And of course, the feast that the Lord throws us is one full of richness and wine.

> But here on this mountain, God-of-the-Angel-Armies will throw a feast for all the people of the world, a feast of the finest foods, a feast with vintage wines, a feast of seven courses, a feast lavish with gourmet desserts. And here on this mountain, God will banish the pall of doom hanging over all peoples, the shadow of doom darkening all nations. Yes, He'll banish death forever. And God will wipe the tears from every face. He'll remove every sign of disgrace from His people, wherever they are. Yes! God says so!
>
> Also at that time, people will say, "Look at what's happened! This is our God! We waited for Him and He showed up and saved us! This God, the one we waited for! Let's celebrate, sing the joys of His salvation. God's hand rests on this mountain!"[238]

True Christianity is a celebration! And we are celebrating something very specific. There is a very specific meal being served—and we must eat it!

> ...Christ, God's Lamb, has been slain for us. So let us feast upon Him....[239]
>
> For Christ, the antitypical Passover Lamb, has been sacrificed for us, and we Christians are to keep a feast which celebrates deliverance from sin.[240]

We are to feast on the sacrifice of Jesus Christ. The table has been set, the Passover Lamb has been given, and the wine has been poured.

This feast is the same as it was for the Israelites when they celebrated the Passover. We are to feast on the Lamb and celebrate our exodus out of the slavery of sin.

We, like the children of Israel, are not to leave anything, but to eat every last bite.[241] We are to eat until we are fattened with grace and cannot move from our position of trust!

+ Famous for Your **BLISS**

When God saved you, He had worldwide fame in mind!

The Lord wants to make His people famous—for their bliss!

> *Said the Eternal to Abram, "Leave your country, leave your kindred, leave your father's house, for a land that I will show you; I will make a great nation of you and bless you and make you famous for your bliss; those who bless you, I will bless, and anyone who curses you I will curse, till all nations of the world seek bliss such as yours."*[242]

The Lord wants to wildly put His fame and divine favor upon His people. He wants to put such joy on them that they are envied by all others. So much so, that everyone in the whole earth seeks the same source of bliss. That Source is Christ Himself and His work on the cross. The river of bliss flows from the slain Lamb.[243]

He is the High Priest of the bliss! *"...Christ arrived as the high priest of the bliss..."*[244] and happy are His people![245]

The people of God should be the most healthy, happy, and holy in the whole world. The Lord wants to use this divine favor to revolutionize the earth by bringing Heaven to it.

We are made famous for our bliss so that we can make the world jealous.

I have spoken much about the needlessness of self-efforts and works, with respect to our acceptance with the Lord; but there are works, holy works, that He produces in and through the believer.

These are outflows of bliss!

The effortlessness of the Gospel should not be misunderstood to be apathy. On the contrary, when such bliss and love come to possess our hearts, we cannot stop the divine flow of holy works.

The heavenly happiness of the Gospel is so strong that we are overcome by the desire to share it! We are possessed by the love of the Gospel. We must give it away!

> ...I couldn't keep from preaching it if I wanted to. I would be utterly miserable....[246]

> ...An overmastering constraint forces me to do it. Ay, woe to me, if I do not proclaim the Glad tidings![247]

The divine love of the Gospel leads us to some of the most dangerous places in the world. It gives us an insatiable hunger to visit the poor and give them our kisses. It makes us throw our arms around all kinds of people, from lepers to terrorists.

This comes not out of self-works or the attempt to gain the approval of God or humanity; it comes out of love.

It all flows out from love!

God loves these works because they come from Him. He prepared them for us to walk in.[248] We are simply walking in His works!

True fruit is truly the work of the Spirit. It is the fruit produced by the spirit within the believer. *"...the fruit of the [Holy] Spirit [the work which His presence within accomplishes]...."*[249]

It is impossible for us to be prideful about these works because they don't come from us. We are simply following the joy of the Gospel.

The Lord wants to use His people to pour out His love. He wants to use us to pour out *His joy*.

It is *His bliss* that is *our fame!* And the Lord wants to use His people, the Church, to intoxicate the earth, so all can join in the singing of the psalm, *"You visited the earth and intoxicated it."*[250]

+ Are You Completely SATISFIED?

Jesus wants us to be completely satisfied on His offering. In ancient times, the fat of the offering was the most delightful and best part.

> The Hebrews were more fond of fat than we are, and their highest idea of festive provision is embodied in the two words, "marrow and fatness."[251]

In Psalm 36, we find a perfect picture of satisfaction upon the fatness and goodness of God.

They will be intoxicated with the fatness of your house, and you will give them to drink of the wadi of your delights.[252]

The word for "intoxicated" here is *ravah* in Hebrew. It means "to be satiated or saturated, to have or drink one's fill, to be drunk, be intoxicated, to drench, to water abundantly, to bathe."[253]

The word for "fatness" in Hebrew is *deshen* and is defined as "the fatty ashes from the victim of the sacrifice."[254]

This can mean nothing less to us than that we are to be abundantly intoxicated, saturated, and satiated upon the richness of the sacrifice of Jesus Christ!

He was the victim of the sacrifice, and it is with His fatness that we are satisfied.

The psalm goes on to say that *"He gives us to drink of the wadi of delights."*

The word for "delights" is the Hebrew word *eden*, which means "delight or pleasure."[255] Yes, He gives us again the drink of Eden, the pleasure of union with God.

The King James Version says that the Lord *"makes them to drink."*[256]

> ...grace makes us to drink by faith, and then our pleasure is of the richest kind. The Lord not only brings us to this river, but makes us to drink: herein we see the condescension of divine love.[257]

I love the Ancient Roots Translinear version of Psalm 36:8: *"Soak them with the butterfat of your house and water them from the riverbed Eden."*

All those who drink from this river become completely satisfied. We are like the priests whose portion is the finest and fattest of the sacrifice.

"I will soak the souls of the priests with butterfat, and satisfy my people with my goodness."[258] Yes, as Christians we are to be completely satisfied. Satisfied upon the abundance of the offering of Christ.

The Gospel of Matthew says:

> *Blessed are those who hunger and thirst for righteousness, for they will be filled.*[259]

This word for "filled" is *chortazo* in Greek and it means "to be fattened."[260]

We are those who are fattened with righteousness!

I love how the Amplified translates this verse:

> *Blessed and fortunate and happy and spiritually prosperous (in that state in which the born-again child of God enjoys His favor and salvation) are those who hunger and thirst for righteousness (uprightness and right standing with God), for they shall be completely satisfied!*[261]

A Christian is one who is completely filled with all the fullness of God, and is inebriated on what He has done for him or her![262]

Christianity on Earth is not a lifetime of hunger but a lifetime of feasting on eternity's riches. They want nothing, lack nothing, and need nothing.

> *Jehovah is my shepherd, I do not lack.*[263]

God, my shepherd! I don't need a thing.[264]

Only the Happy Gospel can fill us to the brim like this!

> Happy is the soul that can drink in the sumptuous dainties of the gospel–nothing can so completely fill the soul.[265]

+ Drinking from the ROCK

In Exodus chapter 17 we see a wonderful picture of the work of the cross. We read that while in their desert journey, the children of Israel thirsted for water.

The Lord spoke to Moses and told him to go ahead of the Israelites until he reached a certain rock. This rock was at Horeb, which is another name for Mount Sinai.

It should be noted that the Lord Himself was standing upon this rock, *"I will stand before thee there upon the rock in Horeb...."*[266]

When Moses reached this rock that was at Horeb (Mount Sinai) he was commanded to take his rod and strike the rock. When Moses did this, water burst out from the rock, so much so that two million Israelites could drink freely.

> This supply of water, on Moses only striking the rock where no water had been before nor has been since, was a most wonderful display of the Divine Power. The water must have been in great abundance to supply two millions of persons, which excluded all possibility of artifice or imposture in the case. The miracle must also

have been of some continuance, no doubt so long as they continued in that neighborhood, which was more than a year.[267]

It wasn't just a few drops that flowed, but rivers that poured out from inside of this rock. *"He brought streams also out of the rock, and caused waters to run down like rivers."*[268] I believe that when Moses struck this rock, multiple streams and rivers flowed out and down the mount of Sinai, and all the Israelites, their children, and all their livestock had ample water for a long while, as the river followed them through the desert.

> The supply of water was as plenteous in quantity as it was miraculous in origin. Torrents, not driblets came from the rocks. Streams followed the camp; the supply was not for an hour or a day. This was a marvel of goodness. If we contemplate the abounding of divine grace we shall be lost in admiration. Mighty rivers of love have flowed for us in the wilderness.[269]

Deuteronomy also tells us that not only water, but honey also came from the rock.[270]

The word for "strike" used in this Scripture in Hebrew is *nakah*. It not only means "to strike" but also "to slay or kill."[271]

The apostle Paul brings us into the full revelation of this portion of Scripture as the following commentary on First Corinthians shows:

> *And all drank the same typical drink: For they drank of water from the typical rock, which water followed them; and that rock was a type of Christ, as the Source of all revelations of God.*[272]

The rock that was struck in the desert was a type and preview of the work that Christ would carry out upon the cross. He was the rock that was struck, and out flowed from Him the spiritual river that all believers drink from—just as when Christ was pierced in His side by the centurion and out flowed water.

> ..."This rock signified Christ, and is therefore called a spiritual Rock [see 1 Cor. 10:4]. He being smitten with Moses' rod, and bearing the curse of the law for our sins, and by the preaching of the Gospel crucified among his people, from him floweth the spiritual drink wherewith all believing hearts are refreshed [see Gal. 3:1]."[273]

Christ Himself said, "*If anyone thirsts* [as did the Israelites in the desert], *let him come to Me and drink.*"[274]

When humankind drinks from this Rock, Christ, they will never thirst again!

We read in another portion of Scripture a similar story.

In Numbers chapter 20, we see again the Israelites' complaints of thirst. They all saw and drank from the miracle previously mentioned.

They needed not complain about their thirst, but simply ask for water. Yet, they did not do this. Though the Israelites' tongues were filled with complaints and unbelief, the Lord in His infinite mercy still provided drink for them.

He again showed Moses a particular rock—most likely the same as the previous one, as the apostle Paul states that it "followed the Israelites"[275] through the desert.

Yet, this time the Lord says only to *"speak to the rock"*[276] and the water will flow. The word *speak* also means to "sing."[277] Moses was to simply sing to the rock and it would pour forth water for all to drink.

But Moses did not do this; he struck the rock twice.

Again, we see the mercies of our Lord on display; even though Moses did not do as he was commanded, the water still flowed. The Lord still provided drink for His children.

For this offense, Moses was disqualified from entering into the Promised Land. Some would say that this is an extremely severe punishment for such a seemingly small crime. But, the Lord saw this not as a small matter.

We read that Moses' sin was that he *"did not believe"*[278] the Lord, and therefore he could not lead the children into the Promised Land.

Again, we must view these Scriptures in the light of Christ and His crucifixion.

These were not just stories of miraculous provision, but were vivid types of Christ's sacrifice, which in this case is the reason for the Lord's severity.

This was no ordinary rock; this Rock was Christ!

And, this Rock need only be struck once. Christ need not be crucified twice. His one sacrifice is sufficient for all time to quench the thirst of the heart of humanity.

When we do not believe that Christ's sacrifice alone is sufficient to produce satisfaction for our hearts, we become guilty of the same unbelief as Moses. If we become dependent upon some work or labor of our own to produce perfect salvation, it is like we are striking the rock again. It is distrust in the crucifixion of Christ.

This may sound harsh, yet remember, so did the punishment of Moses. The Lord is jealous about His Son and His offering!

We need only to speak to this Rock and it will burst with drink. Only a song of praise is required for this well to spring up. Only faith in the work of the cross is able to produce perfect salvation, which is the Promised Land.

Even a quick glance at the epistle of Galatians makes us realize that perfect salvation can only come by faith in the cross. We to whom "Christ has been portrayed clearly as crucified before our eyes,"[279] need to look only to Him for our perfection.

Do not let the bewitchment of religion and unbelief blind you from this!

These stories recorded in Exodus and Numbers stand as witnesses; if we listen, they will speak to us. They tell of Christ's cross and the Lord's jealousy of it. They speak to us about the unending rewards of childlike trust and warn us of the disappointments of unbelief.

Let us not be disqualified by distrusting Him and His way of salvation. But let us sing unending melodies of praise; let the Rock of our salvation burst with drink.

> Come, let us sing to the Lord! Let us shout joyfully to the Rock of our salvation. Let us come to Him with thanksgiving. Let us sing psalms of praise to Him. For the Lord is a great God, a great King above all gods.[280]

YOUR NOTES=

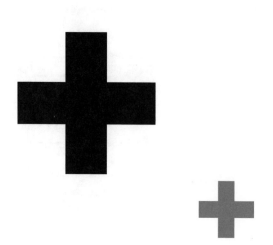

Epilogue

+ EPILOGUE

When presented in its brilliance and its sweetness, we can come to no other conclusion than this—that *the Gospel* is an irresistible drink of joy!

It is revolutionizing and scandalizing.

It shocks us with endless ease.

It is almost too good to be true.

Its goodness is absolutely overwhelming.

It is life-changing.

It is life-giving.

It speaks to us in a language that sometimes we don't understand, but it waits patiently for us to learn.

It is my prayer that in reading this book, you have feasted and have been satiated on the Gospel's glorious goodness.

I hope you have taken deep, wonderful draughts of its fountains.

I hope you have quenched your thirst and found the same joy as I when presented this wonderful grace.

I pray you found the Goodness of the News and its Source.

I pray that you found the Happy Gospel!

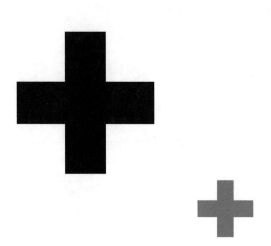

Endnotes

+ ENDNOTES

1. See 1 Timothy 1:11 *Rotherham*.

2. Joseph Henry Thayer, *A Greek-English Lexicon of the New Testament* (New York: Harper & Brothers, 1889).

3. James Strong, LL.D., S.T.D, *Strong's Dictionary of New Testament Words* (Nashville, TN: Thomas Nelson, 1996).

4. W.E. Vine, *Vine's Complete Expository Dictionary of Old and New Testament Words* (Nashville, TN: Thomas Nelson, 1996).

5. Ephesians 2:8 *King James Version*.

6. *Vine's Complete Expository Dictionary.*

7. See Ephesians 2:8.

8. *Vine's Complete Expository Dictionary.*

9. See Romans 6.

10. *Vine's Complete Expository Dictionary.*

11. Ibid.

12. Colossians 2:11 *Amplified.*

13. *Vine's Complete Expository Dictionary.*

14. *Amplified.*

15. *Thayer's Lexicon.*

16. Ibid.

17. See 1 Corinthians 1:30.

18. *Vine's Complete Expository Dictionary.*

19. *Thayer's Lexicon.*

20. Galatians 5:22 *Amplified.*

21. See James 1:27.

22. *The American Heritage Dictionary of the English Language*, Fourth Edition (New York: Houghton Mifflin Company, 2000).

23. Ibid.

24. *Thayer's Lexicon.*

25. Ibid.

26. Genesis 1:1 *Adam Clarke's Commentary on the Bible.*

27. Romans 1:1 *Conybeare*.

28. Romans 1:1 *Wuest*.

29. 1 Timothy 1:11 *Rotherham*.

30. "Commentary on Psalm 126" Charles H. Spurgeon, *The Treasury of David*, 1876.

31. Romans 1:3 *Phillips*.

32. See Galatians 1:6 *Amplified Bible*.

33. C.S. Lewis, *The Weight of Glory*.

34. Isaiah 55:1 *Amplified*.

35. *Strong's Dictionary of New Testament Words*.

36. "Question 1," *The Westminster Larger Catechism*, 1647.

37. Matthew 26:27-28 *King James Version*.

38. See Deuteronomy 12:23.

39. Psalm 23:5 *Douay-Rheims*.

40. St. Cyprian, *Epistles of Cyprian of Carthage*.

41. Robert Farrar Capon, *Between Noon and Three: Romance, Law, and the Outrage of Grace* (Grand Rapids: Wm. B. Eerdmans Publishing Co.), 109-110.

42. Romans 1:4 *Cotton Patch*.

43. See John 8:56.

44. *Strong's* definition for "rejoiced."

45. 1 Peter 1:10-12 *Wuest.*

46. *Vine's Complete Expository Dictionary.*

47. Psalm 68:27 *Douay-Rheims.*

48. Psalm 31:1 *Douay-Rheims.*

49. Matthew 2:10 *Amplified.*

50. Acts 3:10 *Wycliffe.*

51. Luke 5:26 *Amplified.*

52. Mark 16:8 *LITV.*

53. John 20:20 *Amplified.*

54. Acts 10:10 *ERV.*

55. Acts 11:5 *Darby.*

56. Acts 11:5 *Douay-Rheims.*

57. 2 Corinthians 5:13 *Heart of Paul.*

58. Acts 22:17 *Amplified.*

59. Acts 22:17 *ERV.*

60. Jude 24 *Amplified.*

61. Friedrich Wilhelm Gesenius, *Gesenius' Hebrew-Chaldee Lexicon to the Old Testament*, 1846.

62. See Genesis 3:10.

63. Romans 1:5 *A.S. Way.*

64. Romans 1:5 *Barclay.*

65. Revelation 13:8 *God's Word.*

66. Genesis 3:21 *John Wesley's Notes on the Bible.*

67. "Commentary on Psalm 126" Spurgeon, *Treasury of David.*

68. Hebrews 10:19-20 *Wuest.*

69. Romans 6:5 *Cotton Patch.*

70. Romans 6:1-3 *The Message.*

71. Galatians 2:20, *Distilled Bible.*

72. *Vine's Complete Expository Dictionary.*

73. Ibid.

74. 2 Corinthians 5:17a *Wuest.*

75. 2 Corinthians 5:17a *TCNT.*

76. 2 Corinthians 5:17a *Phillips.*

77. 2 Corinthians 5:17a *New English Bible.*

78. 2 Corinthians 5:17b *Conybeare.*

79. 2 Corinthians 5:17b *Knox.*

80. 2 Corinthians 5:17b *Phillips.*

81. 2 Corinthians 5:17b *New English Bible.*

82. Thayer and Smith. *The KJV New Testament Greek Lexicon,* Greek Lexicon entry for *Archaios.*

83. *Vine's Complete Expository Dictionary.*

84. Gerald Hawthorne, Ralph Martin & Daniel Reid, eds., *Dictionary of Paul and His Letters* (Grovers Down, IL: Intervarsity Press, 1993).

85. Colossians 3:9-10 *King James Version.*

86. *Strong's Dictionary of New Testament Words.*

87. Romans 5:14-15 *Jerusalem Bible.*

88. Isaiah 53:11 *Amplified.*

89. Isaiah 43:19 *Amplified.*

90. Ezekiel 36:26 *The Message.*

91. Ephesians 3:19 *Amplified.*

92. See Colossians 2:11.

93. Romans 2:28-29 *Weymouth.*

94. Romans 2:28-29 *A.S. Way.*

95. Romans 2:28-29 *F.F. Bruce.*

96. Romans 2:28-29 *Barclay.*

97. Romans 2:28-29 *Knox.*

98. Ezekiel 36:36 *Adam Clarke's Commentary on the Bible.*

99. Psalm 23:6 *Amplified.*

100. Galatians 5:6 *Stevens.*

101. See Psalm 144:15.

102. Psalm 68:2-3 *The Message.*

103. See Romans 6:6 *Amplified.*

104. Adam Clarke, *Entire Sanctification.*

105. Ephesians 2:10 *Amplified.*

106. Romans 6:13 *Amplified.*

107. Matthew 27:52-53 *Amplified.*

108. Note on 2 Corinthians 5:4 *Weymouth.*

109. Romans 8:30 *Amplified.*

110. See Colossians 2:10 *Amplified.*

111. 1 Corinthians 1:30.

112. See Matthew 20: 1-16.

113. See Deuteronomy 32:13.

114. 1 Corinthians 1:23 *Amplified.*

115. *Thayer's Lexicon.*

116. George Barker Stevens, *The Theology of the New Testament* 412.

117. See Genesis 22:5.

118. Hebrews 11:17,19 *King James Version.*

119. *Vine's Expository Dictionary.*

120. Genesis 22:7-8 *King James Version.*

121. Genesis 22:8 *Adam Clarke's Commentary on the Bible.*

122. Romans 4:2 *The Message.*

123. Genesis 22:14 *Adam Clarke's Commentary on the Bible.*

124. Genesis 22:2 *Adam Clarke's Commentary on the Bible.*

125. Stevens, *Theology of the New Testament,* 403.

126. See Matthew 11:30.

127. See John 13:8.

128. *Thayer's Lexicon.*

129. Matthew 16:24 *Young's Literal Translation.*

130. Matthew 16:24 *Phillips.*

131. Philippians 2:12-13 *A.S. Way.*

132. Ephesians 2:8 *Amplified.*

133. Martin Luther's famous "Tower Experience" written in 1519.

134. See Habakkuk 2:4; Romans 1:17.

135. Romans 1:17 *Cassier.*

136. See Philippians 3:6.

137. Philippians 3:8-9 *A.S. Way.*

138. See 1 Corinthians 1:30.

139. Matthew 5:48.

140. Matthew 5:48 *Adam Clarke's Commentary on the Bible.*

141. Hebrews 9:15 *Stevens.*

142. Hebrews 10:14 *Stevens.*

143. Clarke, *Entire Sanctification.*

144. *Thayer's Lexicon.*

145. *Gesenius' Lexicon.*

146. See Numbers 13:23, the supernatural cluster of grapes carried on a "staff" is a type of Christ's crucifixion.

147. See Numbers 13:33.

148. See Numbers 14:9.

149. Ibid.

150. Numbers 13:33 *Adam Clarke's Commentary on the Bible.*

151. See Leviticus 20:24.

152. See Numbers 14:8.

153. See Joshua 24:13.

154. See Numbers 14:33-34.

155. Hebrews 3:19 *Amplified.*

156. See Deuteronomy 29:5.

157. Numbers 14:24 *Adam Clarke's Commentary on the Bible.*

158. See Hebrews 4:2.

159. Ibid.

160. Psalm 126:1-3 *The Message.*

161. "Commentary on Psalm 126" Spurgeon, *Treasury of David.*

162. Ibid.

163. Psalm 14:7, 53:6 *The Message.*

164. See Galatians 6:14.

165. See Acts 26:24.

166. 2 Corinthians 5:13 *Heart of Paul.*

167. 2 Corinthians 5:13 *Cotton Patch.*

168. Acts 18:5 *Berkeley.*

169. 2 Corinthians 5:14 *Wuest.*

170. 2 Corinthians 5:14 *Weymouth.*

171. 2 Corinthians 5:14 *NEB.*

172. 1 Corinthians 4:1 *Douay-Rheims.*

173. Hawthorne, Martin, Reid, eds., *Dictionary of Paul and His Letters.*

174. Colossians 2:2 *Amplified.*

175. George Barker Stevens, *The Pauline Theology,* 32-43.

176. 2 Corinthians 12:2 *Stevens.*

177. Galatians 1:11 *God's Word.*

178. See Galatians 1:12.

179. See 1 Corinthians 6:17.

180. See Psalm 40.

181. Revelation 5:9.

182. See Colossians 1:13.

183. Colossians 2:11 *Amplified.*

184. Romans 6:11 *The Message.*

185. See Revelation 10:10.

186. See 1 Samuel 14:29 *Douay-Rheims.*

187. Jeremiah 15:16 *ESV.*

188. *Vine's Complete Expository Dictionary.*

189. See 2 Corinthians 5:14.

190. 2 Corinthians 5:14 *Wuest.*

191. 2 Corinthians 5:14 *King James Version.*

192. *Greek Lexicon.*

193. See Galatians 2:20.

194. Romans 7:4 *King James Version.*

195. Romans 7:4 *Wuest.*

196. See Romans 5:20.

197. See Romans 5:20.

198. Romans 5:20 *Phillips.*

199. Hawthorne, Martin, Reid, eds., *Dictionary of Paul and His Letters.*

200. Romans 8:30 *Adam Clarke's Commentary on the Bible.*

201. See Leviticus 23:3,28,31.

202. See Leviticus 23:30.

203. http://www.aish.com/sp/k/48955731.html#; accessed December 1, 2010.

204. *Adam Clarke's Commentary on the Bible.*

205. *David Guzik's Commentaries on the Bible.*

206. See also Psalm 40.

207. Revelation 5:9 *The Exegeses Translation*

208. Genesis 4:4 *King James Version.*

209. *Thayer's Lexicon.*

210. See Hebrews 11:4.

211. Genesis 4:7 *Amplified.*

212. *Hebrew Lexicon.*

213. Ibid.

214. Ibid.

215. Genesis 4:7 *Young's Literal Translation*.

216. Genesis 4:7 *Rotherham*.

217. Revelation 3:20 *King James Version*.

218. Acts 2:37 *New Living Translation*.

219. John 6:29 *New Living Translation*.

220. See 1 Corinthians 12:10.

221. *Thayer's Lexicon*.

222. See Luke 5:37.

223. Habakkuk 3:18 *The Message*.

224. Isaiah 35:10 *The Message*.

225. Juan Gonzalz Arintero, *Song of Songs: A Mystical Exposition* (Tan Books & Pub, 1994).

226. Revelation 5:6 *Wuest*.

227. Isaiah 6:3.

228. Colossians 1:27 *Amplified*.

229. Luke 5:33-34 *Living Bible*.

230. Luke 5:35 *Living Bible*.

231. Romans 6:11 *Amplified*.

232. See Leviticus 16:29; 23:32.

233. Mark 2:20 *Wuest Word Studies*.

234. Deuteronomy 28:47 *God's Word*.

235. Isaiah 58:5-7 *Amplified*.

236. See Luke 14:21-24.

237. 2 Samuel 9:6-11.

238. Isaiah 25:6-10 *The Message*.

239. 1 Corinthians 5:7-8 *Living Bible*.

240. 1 Corinthians 5:7-8 *Stevens*.

241. See Exodus 12:10.

242. Genesis 12:1-3 *Moffatt*.

243. See Revelation 22:1.

244. Hebrews 9:11 *Moffatt*.

245. Psalm 144:15.

246. 1 Corinthians 9:16 *Living Bible*.

247. 1 Corinthians 9:16 *The Way*.

248. See Ephesians 2:10.

249. Galatians 5:22 *Amplified*.

250. Psalm 65:10 *Septuagint*.

251. "Commentary on Psalms 63" Spurgeon, *Treasury of David*.

252. Psalm 36:8 *Septuagint.*

253. "Dictionary and Word Search for *ravah* (Strong's 7301)," *Blue Letter Bible.* 1996–2010.

254. *Gesenius' Lexicon.*

255. Ibid.

256. Psalm 36:8 *King James Version.*

257. "Commentary on Psalm 36" Spurgeon, *Treasury of David.*

258. Jeremiah 31:14 *Ancient Roots.*

259. Matthew 5:6 *New International Version*

260. *Thayer's Lexicon.*

261. Matthew 5:6 *Amplified.*

262. See Ephesians 3:19.

263. Psalm 23:1 *Young's Literal Translation.*

264. Psalm 23:1 *The Message.*

265. "Commentary on Psalms 36" Spurgeon, *Treasury of David.*

266. Exodus 17:6 *King James Version.*

267. Exodus 17:6 *Adam Clarke's Commentary on the Bible.*

268. Psalm 78:16 *King James Version.*

269. "Commentary on Psalm 78" Spurgeon, *Treasury of David*.

270. See Deuteronomy 32:13.

271. *Strong's Dictionary of New Testament Words*.

272. 1 Corinthians 10:4 *James MacKnight Commentary*.

273. Quote in Exodus 17:7 *Adam Clarke's Commentary on the Bible* (quoting a Mr. Ainsworth).

274. John 7:37 *New King James Version*.

275. See 1 Corinthians 10:4.

276. Numbers 20:8 *New King James Version*.

277. "Dictionary and Word Search for dabar" (Strong's 1696), *Blue Letter Bible*.

278. Numbers 20:12 *New King James Version*.

279. See Galatians 3:1.

280. Psalm 95:1-3 *Living Bible*.

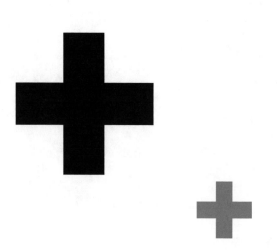

Index

+ INDEX

E

ecstasy 33, 49, 50, 51, 52, 53, 54, 55, 56, 57, 75, 123, 125, 126, 127, 147

eden 167

Eden 55, 56, 167

effortless 73, 78, 109, 112, 115, 136, 137

F

fat 80, 166

flesh 32, 56, 129, 130, 140

freedom 41, 46, 69, 87

G

glorified body 73, 77, 159

glory 31, 48, 51, 92, 96, 111, 144, 159, 160

Gospel 20, 21, 31, 33, 38, 39, 40, 41, 42, 43, 44, 46, 48, 49, 51, 52, 55, 57, 63, 80, 81, 86, 87, 97, 99, 101, 103, 108, 114, 115, 123, 124, 127, 130, 132, 141, 142, 144, 147, 148, 149, 154, 155, 156, 157, 159, 160, 162, 165, 166, 169, 171, 178, 179

grace 31, 41, 42, 46, 47, 48, 58, 67, 98, 101, 129, 138, 139, 142, 145, 164, 167, 170, 179

H

Happy 21, 31, 34, 38, 39, 48, 99, 116, 129, 139, 154, 155, 156, 157, 160, 161, 164, 168, 169, 179

healing 66, 75, 78, 140, 148

health 75, 77, 78

J

joy 33, 39, 40, 42, 43, 44, 45, 46, 48, 49, 50, 51, 52, 57, 62, 71, 72, 73, 81, 94, 115, 116, 117, 126, 127, 131, 142, 143, 144, 154, 155, 156, 157, 158, 159, 161, 164, 166, 178, 179

L

M

N

P

S

+ ABOUT THE AUTHOR

BENJAMIN AND STEPHANIE DUNN+ are carriers of the "Bliss of Salvation." They are two lovers who travel around the world proclaiming the extravagant message of the cross of Jesus Christ. They are absolutely enamored with the mystical love of the glorious Gospel! Through joyous childlike worship and demonstration, and a message of the incalculable riches of Jesus Christ, Benjamin and Stephanie minister a massive drink of the Truth. God forbid that they boast about anything or anyone but the cross of Jesus Christ, who is the river of pleasure!

He makes me to drink of the river called pleasure
(Psalm 36:8).

For teachings and resources from Benjamin Dunn please visit:

www.joyrevolution.com

+ questions or event IDEAS?

Benjamin and Stephanie would enjoy ministering at your church, conference, or event. Please contact them with a few details, and you will receive a prompt response.

+ scheduling

Christy Russell, Assistant to Benjamin and Stephanie Dunn
Email: christy@joyrevolution.com
Telephone: 1-224-475-5958

+ primary contact INFORMATION

Joy Revolution Ministries
4415 Diamond St., Capitola, CA 95010
Email: christy@joyrevolution.com

In the right hands, This Book will Change Lives!

Most of the people who need this message will not be looking for this book. To change their lives, you need to put a copy of this book in their hands.

> *But others (seeds) fell into good ground, and brought forth fruit, some a hundred-fold, some sixty-fold, some thirty-fold* (Matthew 13:8).

Our ministry is constantly seeking methods to find the good ground, the people who need this anointed message to change their lives. Will you help us reach these people?

> *Remember this—a farmer who plants only a few seeds will get a small crop. But the one who plants generously will get a generous crop* (2 Corinthians 9:6).

EXTEND THIS MINISTRY BY SOWING
3 BOOKS, 5 BOOKS, 10 BOOKS, OR MORE TODAY,
AND BECOME A LIFE CHANGER!

Thank you,

Don Nori Sr., Publisher
Destiny Image
Since 1982